POLKA KING

POLKA KING

The Life and Times of Polka Music's Living Legend

JIMMY STURR

BenBella Books, Inc.
Dallas, Texas

BenBella
BenBella Books, Inc.
10300 N. Central Expressway
Suite #530
Dallas, TX 75231
www.benbellabooks.com
Send feedback to feedback@benbellabooks.com

Printed in the United States of America
10 9 8 7 6 5 4 3 2 1

Library of Congress Cataloging-in-Publication Data

Sturr, Jimmy.
Polka King : the life and times of polka music's living legend / by Jimmy Sturr.
    pages cm
ISBN 978-1-937856-34-2 (hardcover) -- ISBN 978-1-937856-35-9 (e-book) 1.
Sturr, Jimmy. 2. Musicians--United States--Biography. 3. Polkas--United
States--History and criticism. I. Title.
ML419.S83A3 2013
784.18′844092--dc23
[B]

                                                                                      2013001227

Editing by Erin Kelley
Copyediting by Lisa Miller
Proofreading by Chris Gage and Kristin Vorce
Cover design by Sarah Dombrowsky
Text design and composition by Elyse Strongin, Neuwirth & Associates, Inc.
Printed by Berryville Graphics, Inc.

Distributed by Perseus Distribution
perseusdistribution.com

To place orders through Perseus Distribution:
Tel: 800-343-4499
Fax: 800-351-5073
E-mail: orderentry@perseusbooks.com

CONTENTS

Contents

FOREWORD
by Willie Nelson

I was in sixth grade when I landed my first professional gig, and it might surprise you that it wasn't with a country band or a blues group or a gospel ensemble. No, my first paying job was with John Raycjeck's Bohemian Polka Band. That's right, folks. Willie Nelson made his debut with a polka band . . . and I'm proud of it. Playing those waltzes and polkas all around Texas wasn't a particularly lucrative endeavor—I earned the less-than-princely sum of eight dollars per night—but the many crowds' love for the music more than made up for the small paycheck. Little wonder that there's always been a big place in my heart for polka music.

Fast-forward to 1996, when I received a call from Mr. Jimmy Sturr, a polka man from the great town of Florida, New York, in the great county of Orange. Now, being that I had an affinity for polka, I was well aware of who Jimmy was. (If memory serves, he'd won seven of his eighteen Grammy Awards by then.) When he asked me to guest on a record that came to be called *Polka! All Night Long*, I said, "Absolutely," without a second's hesitation. Turned out, that session was a blast. Jimmy's adoration for the music, his band's passionate energy, and those inimitable polka beats brought me right back to my childhood. Thus began a musical friendship that endures to this day.

I recorded four more albums with Jimmy and the band, each more fun than the last; I'm proud to say all of them won Grammy Awards. Naturally, I had to get Jimmy on the Farm Aid bill; he graced our stage in 2005, 2006, and 2007, and I had the distinct pleasure of performing with him all three years. I say pleasure because as much of a blast as it was to record with Jimmy and his Orchestra, it was that much more fun to sing some polkas live, in front of tens of thousands of fans. Brought me right on back to my tenure with the Bohemian Band.

All of this is why I'm thrilled that Jimmy has finally put pen to paper to tell his story. *The Polka King* is the tale of a small-town boy made good—that's something I personally can relate to—a man who brought the music he grew up with and loved to the masses, simply because it was in his blood. Jimmy has traveled the world and has probably played more gigs for more people than any other polka musician in the history of mankind, so if there's any gentleman who understands that life and those sounds, it's Jimmy.

Even if the only thing you know about polka is rolling out the barrel and having a barrel of fun, you'll enjoy Jimmy's book, because it's not just about music. It's about working hard and bringing your dreams to fruition. It's about the ups and downs of making your living as an artist. And, most important, it's about people . . . and Jimmy Sturr is good people.

FOREWORD
by Bobby Vinton

Like me, Jimmy Sturr is a workingman.

He works with his band. He works with his record label. He works with his television show. He works with his radio show. He works with his multitude of business ventures. However, the one thing he works at the hardest is keeping polka alive. And this particular work is *crucial*, because polka has been slowly fading from the mainstream for years now. I couldn't tell you why—after all, it's party music, and parties will always be in fashion, right? But if it wasn't for Jimmy's tenacity, commitment, and talent, I don't think polka music would have even the level of popularity it does today. Thanks in part to the force of his personality, I'm certain that polka will live on forever.

I first heard about Jimmy when I was performing up at the Concord Resort Hotel in the Catskills, a venue that I've always enjoyed for its great stage, great sound, and great audiences. Jimmy came to the show and somehow sweet-talked his way backstage. After he introduced himself—it's possible he referred to himself as "The Polka King," but don't hold me to that—he told me how much he's always enjoyed my music and then reeled off the names of his favorite songs of mine, one right after the other: "Roses Are Red," "Blue Velvet," "There! I've Said It Again," "Mr. Lonely," "My Melody of Love," and so on. But then he started naming some of my lesser-known tunes, tunes like "Petticoat White," "Red Roses for Mom," "Why Don't They Understand," "I'll Make You My Baby," and "Let Me Love You Goodbye." And then he blew me away when he began to dissect my 1981 LP, *Polka Album*. He explained that the way I approached turning pop tunes like The Beatles' "Ob-La-Di, Ob-La-Da" and the standard "That's Amore" made a huge impact on him, and he mentioned that he had a couple of the tunes I recorded in his repertoire, specifically "Pennsylvania Polka," "Too Fat Polka," and "Hoop-Dee-Doo." Then, best of all, he told me how much he loved what I called my "Polka Memories Medley," because several years back he himself had recorded a couple of albums filled with similar medleys. He then went on to explain that one of those albums had seventy-seven songs, and the other featured sixty-six. Finally, he told me how important *my* style of entertainment was to *his* style of entertainment and how he appreciated my ability to reach the people while staying true to my musical roots. I couldn't help but be impressed with the extent of his knowledge, his intelligence, and his warmth. That was about thirty-five years ago. We've been friends ever since.

I feel that the main reason Jimmy Sturr has been able to keep the polka industry thriving is that he's added a dash of contemporary showmanship. Yes, Jimmy Sturr and His Orchestra is a polka band, but it's not just a band that plays polkas. Jimmy offers his listeners—believe me, the man has a *lot* of listeners (if you're buying this book, you're probably one of them)—a whole bunch of variety, the kind of variety that you don't get from many bands, regardless of their chosen genre.

Unlike the majority of the gentlemen who make a living performing and recording polkas, Jimmy is smart enough to invite musicians from other styles to join him in the studio. (That may seem like an obvious route to take, but if it's so obvious, why is Jimmy the only one taking it?) He'll incorporate rock and roll and country and Cajun and pop and jazz and bluegrass and folk, yet he'll never lose that two-beat polka sound. This, I think, is why Jimmy's records are so interesting to the voters who have bestowed upon him all those Grammy Awards. That he displays this unique skill on a weekly television show, which is watched by hundreds of thousands of people, speaks further to his musical and business acumen.

I've been lucky enough to join Jimmy and his band on a number of his polka cruises. His audiences are unbelievably fun, respectful, and happy, and it's always wonderful to see these folks getting intoxicated by music rather than alcohol. Not that there isn't alcohol present—after all, it *is* a polka cruise, and polka is, for many people, music to drink by—but the libations weren't necessary to make the cruise special. A good time would've been had by all, even if the strongest drink on the ship had been Coca-Cola.

When Jimmy retires—and hopefully that won't be for many, many years—I honestly don't know how the polka industry will survive. He's the only one I know of who moves the music forward with every recording. Young musicians need to note that because the polka torch must be carried on. Polka wasn't born *in* America, but it is *of* America; if it fades into the sunset, the music world will be worse off for it. But as long as Jimmy Sturr is on a stage or in a recording studio, I'm confident that polka will continue to thrive.

FOREWORD
by Bill Anderson

Jimmy Sturr is one of those people whom I don't remember not knowing. There are people in your life you feel like have been there forever. That's Jimmy.

Early in our relationship, he booked Porter Wagoner and me to play at a fair in Pennsylvania. Or maybe New Jersey. Or possibly New York. But it doesn't really matter where. He must've been about fifteen, sixteen, seventeen years old, just your average teenager, booking big-time country music shows. Years later, he told me that he made a good bit of money from these things. If you had to describe Jimmy in one word, that word would be "entrepreneur."

The next time I recall our paths crossing was at Newark Symphony Hall in Newark, New Jersey. Jimmy came down from his home in Florida, New York, just like any other fan. I would've gotten him a ticket, but I guess he wanted to support me. That night he sealed our relationship with his fascination for my top-of-the-line Silver Eagle tour bus. Right there, standing in front of the bus, Jimmy said, "Someday, Bill, someday I'm gonna get me one of those. I'm gonna have my name right on the side of a tour bus, just like you." Sure enough, he ended up with his own Silver Eagle, and his own sign. He loves that bus so much that sometimes he'll pick up his fans and take them to his shows. How can you not like that?

The thing that impressed me about Jimmy's approach to polka was his ability to introduce all types of music into the mix. It was still polka, of course, but there were touches of Cajun, bluegrass, and country music. It has a broader scope than I ever thought a polka band could have. Before I heard him, while I liked polka music, it wasn't something I wanted to listen to for hours on end. But the way Jimmy's band members play it, with their sharp arrangements and their ability to connect with an audience, well, give me a few Jimmy Sturr records and a cool drink, and I'll see you tomorrow.

Not only are we great friends but we're great musical associates. Aside from our trips to the studio, I joined him and the Orchestra for three of their infamous Christmas tours. He was always open to collaboration. One year I brought both the steel guitar player and the lead guitar player from my band, and he didn't even blink. There are a lot of artists out there—especially artists of Jimmy's stature—who'd feel threatened if one of their special guests tried to toss his musicians into the stew, but not Jimmy. It was a wonderful melding of our respective styles, and, as far as he was concerned, if it made the crowd happy, he was happy.

Jimmy's the kind of guy who ends up in odd situations. One time, I recall he booked both of our bands to play an outdoor festival in his hometown. Now Florida is not a booming metropolis by any stretch of the imagination, something of which Jimmy was well aware. Knowing there might not be a restaurant to our liking, he told me, "Listen, the show starts at six, so after your soundcheck, bring the band over to my place and we'll have a nice lunch. I'll throw some steaks on the grill, and we'll have a great time."

That sounded wonderful, so when we were all done, I hauled my five band members—two girls and three guys—over to Jimmy's house. He got us a few drinks, sat us down in the backyard, and we started yakking. And yakking. And yakking some more. I looked at my watch and, noticing it was getting close to show time, I started getting nervous because there wasn't any food being cooked. For that matter, the grills weren't even lit. I said to Jimmy, "If we're gonna eat, we'd probably better start moving in that direction."

He said, "You're right," then got up and walked over to a freezer that was situated in his garage, reached in, pulled out a dozen steaks, tossed them to the girls in my band, and said, "It's getting late. You'd better cook these. We've gotta go to the show." The girls looked at the steaks, which were frozen and as hard as a rock. After a second, he started laughing that laugh of his, and we all followed suit. I don't think those grills ever got lit.

Jimmy and I also played together on several of those luxury cruises of his. I loved those things. (In case you didn't know, Jimmy owns his own travel agency and, every so often, packages polka cruises . . . just like every other eighteen-time Grammy winner.) One day we docked in Cozumel, Mexico, and once we hit land, Jimmy said, "We can't go to Cozumel without me showing you Carlos'n Charlie's. That is one wild and crazy place." Carlos'n Charlie's is the kind of bar where there's a pitcher of margaritas on your table before you even sit down. And if there's not a pitcher on the table, it'll be one of the waitresses, dancing her pretty little head off.

I have to mention that in Cozumel, the ships don't dock right on the shore because the water's too shallow. They weigh anchor about fifty feet from the mainland and ferry you to the beach in little boats called tenders; when you're ready to get back on the ship, they ferry you right on back.

It turned out that on the day of our trip to Carlos'n Charlie's, there were two cruise ships anchored out in the water. One was ours. One, naturally, wasn't.

Now I knew we had to perform that night, so I went easy on the margaritas. Jimmy, on the other hand, had one more drink than he should have, which is probably why, after our afternoon festivities came to a close, he got into the wrong tender. Jimmy later told me that when he got onto the wrong cruise ship, he thought, "Wow, nothing here looks familiar," and it took him a few beats to realize that he wasn't where he was supposed to be.

I don't know how he did it, but he sweet-talked one of those tender drivers into paddling him over to his ship. But that's Jimmy Sturr for you: a guy who appreciates a good time, but will do whatever is necessary to get to his show, because for Jimmy, it's all about the fans—and the polka.

POLKA KING

INTRODUCTION

An Irishman in Poland

When I made my first trip to Poland in 1985, the country was still under Communist rule, and it showed. Martial law had been lifted less than two years before, but you could still feel the sense of oppression on every corner. The economy was a disaster, and the badly stocked stores, dirty streets, and empty restaurants reflected that. Warsaw in particular was under a cloud of despair.

But I was invited there to play some American-brand polka for the people, to make the country's music fans feel *good*, and nothing—*nothing*—was going to stop me.

As had been the case for the past five or so years, I liked to put together polka travel packages. For one flat rate, a fan could get transportation to and from the city we were traveling to, a hotel room, and tickets to all the shows, plus the opportunity to hang out with Jimmy Sturr and His Orchestra (that alone was worth the price of admission, if you ask me), but the majority of those shindigs were in New York, New Jersey, and Connecticut; once in a while, we'd make our way up to Massachusetts. This trip to Warsaw, Poland, was far and away the farthest and most expensive tour we'd ever put together. I was hopeful that it would be fun and fruitful for all, but I was aware of the problems Poland was going through, so I had a sense of trepidation during the airplane ride over, tempering my sense of nervous but excited anticipation.

When we landed at the Warsaw Chopin Airport—an unsightly place that made LaGuardia look appealing—we proudly had 550 American polka fanatics in tow. (It took three airplanes to haul us across the Atlantic, and I wouldn't be surprised if it was the biggest United States-to-Poland polka transport of all time.) I was the first person off the airplane on that cloudy, rainy Saturday morning. When I set foot on the tarmac, three little girls met me, each holding a giant bouquet of roses, each wearing their prettiest dress and a warm, hospitable smile. Behind the beaming children stood several stern-looking government officials, clad in crisply pressed, nondescript suits. After the girls handed me the flowers and gave me their sweet little greeting in Polish, the government types wordlessly led me into the airport and down a long hallway, a hallway that, disconcertingly enough, was nowhere near the customs area. They took me through a side door, stuck me in a disturbingly ordinary car—and I say "disturbingly" because their silence and seriousness made me feel as if there was the tiniest chance I'd be kidnapped, and an ordinary car would be harder to identify than, say, a Polski Fiat—and carted me through town. Sitting beside me in the backseat was a frowning, matronly looking woman, who ended up shadowing me for the entire trip. As it turned out, I wasn't kidnapped or thrown in jail or sold off to the highest bidder, but rather brought to my downtown hotel. It wasn't the prettiest building I'd ever seen, but it was warm, dry, and safe, and that was all I needed. I wasn't there to vacation. I was there to entertain.

Our first concert was scheduled for Monday evening, at the Palace of Culture and Science in downtown Warsaw. The palace is a sprawling, impressive structure—ornate and classic looking, albeit drab and a tad dingy—that too few people outside of Poland know about. I suspect part of the reason the country doesn't trumpet it as a tourist attraction is that it was designed and built by the Soviets in the early 1950s, when the Communist Party was at the height of its power. The fact that it was originally called the Josef Stalin Palace of Culture and Science probably didn't help matters.

The soundcheck and preconcert preparation went off without a hitch. The entire band was eager to get moving—this was, after all, one of the biggest concerts in the long, storied history of Jimmy Sturr and His Orchestra—so by the time showtime rolled around, we were on a hair trigger.

Right before we were to take the stage, a gentleman snuck up behind me and barked, "Mr. Sturr!" I turned around and found myself face-to-face with the director of the Palace of Culture and Science. When my heart started beating again, I shook the unsmiling gentleman's hand and asked, "Can I help you?"

"Yes," he grunted, "you can very much help me." He pulled a piece of paper from his breast pocket, unfolded it, then continued, "Before you begin your show, we need to go over this list. There are certain songs that we insist you not play."

Was the government of Poland really going to put restrictions on polka? After all, it *was* Poland, which many consider the birthplace of the music. "What songs are those, sir?"

Reading from the paper, he said, "'The Star-Spangled Banner,' 'God Bless America,' 'The Battle Hymn of the Republic,' 'Dixie,' 'Don't Tread on Me,' 'Stars and Stripes Forever,' 'Home on the Range,' 'Lift Every Voice and Sing,' and anything by Metallica." I could be wrong about the Metallica part. But I could also be right.

"Don't worry," I said. "None of that material is in our repertoire, sir," I said, "so we won't have any problems." Apparently satisfied, he gave me a curt nod and went on his merry way.

The first half of the show went beautifully. The sound in the hall was decent, we played pretty darn well, and everybody in the crowd, from the United States and Poland alike, seemed to be having a great time. At intermission, a shambling, genial-looking gentleman sauntered into the dressing room, stuck out his hand, and said, "John Davis, United States Ambassador to Poland." After we shook hands, he said, "Great show, Jimmy, terrific stuff. It's as good, or maybe even better, than anything you'd hear out here. Can't wait for the second half. So how do you like Poland so far?" Before I could answer, he put his index finger to his lip, pointed to the ceiling, shook his head, and mouthed, "They're listening. Be nice."

I gave him the biggest smile in my arsenal and said, "Mr. Ambassador, I *love* Poland! The people have been nothing but wonderful, the accommodations are clean, and the food has been terrific." (The only thing I lied about was the food. That afternoon, the restaurant at the hotel served me a steak that had probably been sitting under a heat lamp since the Wladyslaw Raczkiewicz administration.) "Do *you* enjoy it here, Mr. Ambassador?"

"Jimmy, Poland is the most wonderful place on the planet. I've been here since 1983, and I can't imagine living anywhere else. Love everything about it—*everything*." He then walked out of the dressing room and motioned me to follow. When we were in the hallway, he leaned into me and whispered, "Watch what you say, Jimmy. Almost every place you'll be taken to is bugged—your hotel, your transportation, the bathrooms, *every-thing*. And you know that grouchy-looking lady who's been following you around? She's KGB."

While this was surprising and strange, none of this clandestine spy business particularly bothered me. I hadn't said anything disparaging about the country to anybody. I probably *wouldn't* be saying anything disparaging, because other than the food, I thought Poland, while not quite heaven on earth, wasn't bad at all. It was a new experience for me, and I planned to embrace it on every level, to focus on the good and ignore the bad. I gave John a smile and said, "Don't you worry one bit, Mr. Ambassador. I don't want to be deported, so I'll watch myself."

When we took the stage for the second half of the show, I *really* looked at the entire audience for the first time that night. (Sometimes when you're on a strange stage in a strange land, you focus more on the music and less on the crowd, at least until you get your bearings.) I noticed that way up in the third balcony, up against the back wall, there were probably twenty to twenty-five armed and uniformed soldiers, marching back and forth, back and forth. Unlike the bugs that the ambassador warned me about, that was disconcerting. I was no stranger to guns (I went to a military academy and spent some time in the army and the National Guard, after all), but it's not every day that you see weaponry at a polka show. I made a conscious effort to ignore the soldiers and focus on the listeners.

Aside from the military men, there were just under three thousand people in the audience that night, five hundred–plus of whom were, as noted, part of our group, and several hundred of whom were Polish relatives of both our tour guests and my band. One of the guys in our group had some family members come to the show, and the only way they could get there was via a ten-hour train ride. (It turned out that they left almost immediately after our performance. Think about that for a second. They rode twenty hours for two hours of polka and a few minutes with a family member they barely knew. That was dedication.) As the show progressed, the vibe in the room became warmer, deeper, and more emotional. I could feel the outpouring of love for us and our music radiating all the way from the back of the room.

Right before our closing number, I leaned into the microphone said, "You know what, my new friends? It's a shame that the whole world can't be with us in this hall, just watching people from two countries, regardless of their political views, sitting together and laughing together and crying together and singing together." After the translator told the audience members what the heck I'd just said, they gave us a wild ovation, after which we launched into the Polish national anthem. After the final note of the song faded into the ozone, I turned to the band and, before I could chicken out, said, "'God Bless America,' key of G. Go!"

Four bars in, much to my surprise, the place went nuts. The folks we'd brought over started singing along, while their Polish brethren clapped and whistled their approval. I don't know what I expected, but it sure wasn't that.

After a whopping four encores, I hustled offstage toward my dressing room. Before I could even turn the corner, the director of the Palace of Culture and Science snuck up behind me and barked, "Mr. Sturr!"

Fortunately, I didn't have any water in my mouth.

At that moment, my overriding thought was, "I hope the Polish prison food is better than the Polish hotel food." I took a deep breath, turned around, and was greeted with a sight that I'll never forget—the cranky-looking liaison had tears in his eyes. He threw his arm around me, pulled me in tight, and said, "Mr. Sturr, this was one of the greatest performances I've ever seen."

So not only was I not arrested but I had somehow managed to touch somebody who I never in a million years could have imagined touching. I figured that with all the clandestine behavior, the hidden listening devices, and the armed guards, anybody in charge of anything in Poland probably had a heart of stone, but boy, was I wrong about that one. The director's reaction almost knocked me on my backside. I mean, who'd have thought a kid from a tiny, one-stoplight town in the Northeast could have a Communist government official tearing up from just a couple hours of polka.

1

The Beginning

Much to his undoubted chagrin and frustration, my father was drafted into the military while my mother was still pregnant, which is why I was born in 1941 in my mother's hometown of Springfield, Massachusetts, which is right down the road from the Basketball Hall of Fame, by the way, rather than the diminutive, two-square-mile town of Florida, New York, my father's hometown, and their place of residence when they got married. It had to have been hard on my mother, being uprooted from her new home and having her first child without her husband on the scene. But my mother was a tough lady, and I'm sure she handled it with grace and courage. After my father finished his tour of duty, we resettled in the town of Florida, and my parents bought the house across the street from the home in which my father was born.

I've lived in that very house ever since and have no plans to leave; if you ever visit me in Florida, you'll understand why. It's a lovely town, quiet and tranquil, filled with nice restaurants and nicer people. (And in 2010, we even lost our status as a one-stoplight town when they put up a second one.) Best of all, I know everybody, and everybody knows me. In every sense of the word, it is my home. I've been lucky enough to travel across the country countless times and perform all over the world, but I wouldn't want to live anywhere other than Florida. Either I was born a small-town boy, or I've become one over time, and the thought of living in a big city doesn't do it for me. And besides, depending on traffic, Manhattan is only a ninety-ish-minute drive away. Why would I want to be anywhere else?

The Florida population back when I was a kid was around 1,500, so there was only one school, the S.S. Seward Institute. If you went to Seward, you were there from kindergarten to high school graduation. (I should mention that if you're ever in Florida, you'll see the name Seward a whole bunch because it was the birthplace of William Henry Seward. Seward, who lived from 1801 to 1872, was arguably one of the finest politicians of his era. He was the twelfth governor of New York, served as secretary of state under both Abraham Lincoln and Andrew Johnson, was an outspoken opponent of slavery, and, most notably, spearheaded the purchase of Alaska from the Russians in 1867. Yes, a guy from Florida bought Alaska. If he'd have played accordion in a polka band, good ol' William Henry Seward would've been *perfect*.) However, Seward Institute wasn't named after the former governor, but rather his father, who started the school back in 1846.

The Seward Institute was just up the street from my house—*everything* in Florida was just up the street from my house, if you want to get technical about it—so I was able to walk to and from school each day, all by myself. (Another reason that my small town trumps your big city: Parents can let their children wander the streets without worrying. The only concern these days is that after a heavy snow, you have to keep your eye peeled for a speeding snowmobile.) Right across the street from the school stood the Lyceum, a bowling alley that, up until I was in sixth grade, used to be an auditorium. When it got converted, we couldn't have been more thrilled because the school's two physical education teachers put their heads together and decided that bowling was an excellent way to burn calories, so we spent many a gym class knocking down pins. (The Lyceum is now my office, my polka headquarters, and the home of the Jimmy Sturr Travel Agency.)

Here's what it was like to live in Florida: Two or three blocks down from the Lyceum stood a hardware store, right on Main Street. It was a three-story building, on top of which sat an enormous speaker. Each and every December, without fail, the hardware store's owner would fire up his record player and pipe Christmas music through those speakers, music that could be heard and enjoyed throughout the entire town. Listening to "Jingle Bells" or "Winter Wonderland" on your way to or from school, while seeing snowmobiles cutting a swath over the freshly fallen snow, just made you feel good. *Everybody* in Florida had a snowmobile—I got my first one when I turned sixteen—and there weren't any laws governing when or where you could drive them. Whenever it snowed at night, you'd see a dozen or so of them zipping up and down Main Street, stopping at one bar, then moving on to the next. I'll admit that the barhopping looked like a whole lot of fun to my teenage self, but knowing what I know now, I would never drive a snowmobile while intoxicated, nor should you.

I was a good kid, in part because my father was a strict but benevolent disciplinarian, and, in part, because I was just a good kid. I played every sport my school had to offer, specifically basketball, baseball, and soccer (unfortunately, they didn't offer football), and also took to the ice with our town's hockey team. But sports was only one of my favorite pastimes. The other was music. And that started *very* early on.

Our next-door neighbor, Mrs. Schmerhorn, was not only my first-grade teacher but from grades one through three, she taught me piano. I enjoyed banging away on her keyboard, but

Jimmy (left) at age four with cousins Judy Haley and Jay Reed.

it didn't particularly inspire me. In retrospect, it's possible that I didn't take to piano because Mrs. Schmerhorn was teaching me more exercises than songs. Parents and music teachers take note: If you want your children to take to their instruments, make sure you give them some context. Yes, they need to learn their scales, but they also have to learn *why* they're learning their scales. This is probably why I didn't stick with piano. But music wasn't about to let me go that easily, because music was in our house.

During an assembly on my first day of third grade, the principal, Mr. McLain, said, "Okay, kids, show of hands. How many of you have a musical instrument at home?" Two seconds after my hand shot into the air, he asked, "What kind of instrument do you have, Mr. Sturr?"

"A saxophone, sir. It's my dad's."

"A saxophone, eh? Well, you go ahead and get that saxophone! Go get it right now!"

My father played sax around town, sometimes with a dance group, sometimes with a marching band. When I was five or six years old, that instrument was always upstairs in our attic; every so often, I'd sneak up the stairs, pick up the shiny, curvy instrument, and pretend I was wailing away. I'd never actually blow; I'd just place my lips around the mouthpiece and finger the keys, imagining that I was surrounded by a roomful of people dancing. It was considerably more enjoyable than plinking and plunking out another étude for Mrs. Schmerhorn.

I had no idea why the principal wanted me to get the sax — maybe it was simply for show-and-tell — nor did I know what I was going to do with it when I returned, but I was nonetheless thrilled. "Yes, sir!" I said, standing up and hustling to the door. "I'll be right back!" It took me about three minutes to sprint home, two minutes to convince my mother to let me borrow my dad's sax, then another four minutes to sprint back. All my classmates oohed and aahed over that glittering saxophone; the principal and my teacher beamed at me as if I were the star pupil. Even though I didn't play a single note, that was, in some ways, the beginning of my life, because from that moment on, my life was all about music.

That very week I started taking private sax lessons, which weren't all that thrilling, although they were more exciting than the piano lessons, since I finally learned some actual songs. It was slow going, but I stuck with it, because I was pretty sure that if I got good, it could lead to . . . *something*. Knowing my dad's work with his bands, I was aware that a guy from Florida could play for adoring crowds (for a burgeoning ham like me, playing for adoring crowds sounded pretty great), but I didn't know how to get there. That didn't stop me from trying both the sax and the clarinet, the saxophone's first cousin, which I took up a couple years later.

Eventually, I began to improve, and the more I improved, the more I enjoyed playing; the more I enjoyed playing, the more I appreciated the polka music that flew from virtually every radio in town. The music's stomping beats and raucous feel hit me on a gut level and gave me something to aspire to. (I finally began to understand how those boring études and overly simple melodies I practiced time and again could be useful; if you know how to do simple stuff, it's easier to do the complex stuff.) Polka became part of my daily life. Polka was in my blood.

All which was why, when I was eleven years old, I started my very first band.

I pitched the idea to our choral teacher, Mrs. Hansen, who gave me a hearty endorsement, dubbed us the Melody Makers, and offered to help us in any way she possibly could. Under Mrs. Hansen's supervision, we practiced and practiced and practiced some more, usually after school, sometimes in my living room, and sometimes in the school's music room. Eventually, we got pretty darn good . . . or at least I thought so at the time. It's probably best for everybody that no tapes of those early rehearsals exist. If I were to place a wager, I'd bet we sounded exactly like what we were: a bunch of eager kids joyously stumbling through a repertoire of simple polkas.

I still remember each and every one of those guys. The accordion player—and he was a good one, even back then—was named Dave Hawkins; Dave still lives not too far from my house and has traded in the squeeze box for a real estate business. Our drummer was Tommy Greco, a great guy who ultimately became a police inspector in Middletown, New York; he's now enjoying his retirement in one of the Carolinas, hopefully banging on his kit every once in a while. Our trumpeters were Paul Ketterer and Corky Palmer, and those guys could blow *loud*, believe me. Finally, there were the Melody Makers' two Polish members (worth noting because so much of polka culture originated in Poland), drummer Walt Miloszewski and Tommy Regelski. A terrific piano player, Tommy was the only Melody Maker other than yours truly who went on to have a career in music, specifically that of a professor at his alma mater, SUNY Fredonia. I sometimes wonder if he thinks about those numerous rehearsals of ours when he's shaping and molding the minds of New York's up-and-coming young musicians.

The Melody Makers' auspicious debut took place at one of our school's monthly Parent Teacher Association meetings, a job that came to me the way many jobs in the music industry come about—connections. In this case my connection was my mother, who was the PTA president. (My father, it should be noted, was the president of the school board, which I'm sure didn't hurt our cause either.) I don't remember our set list, and, as was the case with our rehearsals, the performance wasn't documented on

Ninth grade classmates at Seward High School. From left to right (back row): Eddie Szulewski, Conrad Matuszewski, Tommy Regelski, Jimmy Sturr, and Frankie Shanley. (Front row) Barbara (Sobkowiak) Matuszewski, Rose (Hink) Weslowki, Pat (Sullivan) Jessup, Pat Stzendor, and Rita (Gailie) Rich.

tape. I'm certain, however, that the PTA gave the Melody Makers a wonderful reception. The only downside to the job was that we didn't get paid!

By the time I hit junior high school, I changed the name of the band from the Melody Makers to Jimmy Sturr and the Golden Bells Orchestra. Why? Well, because back then, it seemed like almost every polka band in the great Northeast had a "Bell" in its name. For instance, the great Gene Wisniewski's band was called the Harmony Bells Orchestra, Bernie Witkowski's terrific unit was known as the Silver Bells Orchestra, and good ol' Joe Resetar led the Liberty Bell Orchestra. Why all the bells? No clue. And I never asked. But I figured if bells were good enough for Gene Wisniewski, Bernie Witkowski, and Joe Resetar, then bells were good enough for Jimmy Sturr.

I don't know whether it was because we were that good or that cheap, but for whatever reason, the Golden Bells were hired to play a bunch of the well-attended local street festivals, as well as the occasional Polish wedding. We didn't work as much as we would've liked, however, not because we weren't professional sounding, or because of our ages, but because the Golden Bells Orchestra wasn't the only polka band in the area. As I learned over the next several years, Florida and the surrounding towns and villages comprised one of the great polka music hotbeds in the Northeast.

The most popular group in our area was called the Gay Musicians, which played the majority of the high school dances and seemingly all of the weddings, with an orchestra led by a man named Joe Zack a close second. Joe was so obsessed with music (almost as obsessed as me) that he eventually opened a record shop in which almost 90 percent of the albums were polka, most of which were on Dana Records.

Right now you're probably asking yourself, "Why were there so many polka bands in the Florida, New York, area? And who the heck is Gene Wisniewski? And what the heck is Dana Records?" Well, take a seat, my friends, because I'm about to give you a brief history of polka.

2

Jimmy Sturr's Brief History of Polka

Jimmy Sturr's brief history of polka can't officially begin without Jimmy Sturr's brief history of Florida.

Founded in 1760 by some intrepid, forward-thinking Anglo-European colonists and incorporated in 1946, Florida, New York, is the undisputed "Onion Capital of the World," despite what those big talkers in Vidalia, Georgia, or Oneida Lake, New York, have to say about it. Florida is covered with onion farms, many of which are heavy with what's called black dirt, a type of dirt whose properties make it the perfect birthing place for perfect onions. Even today, it seems like you can't drive a country block without running into an enormous onion farm . . . or two . . . or three.

When all those colonists came from Europe to work in the black dirt, they brought their lives and traditions with them, and by that I mean their traditional recipes, their favored styles of clothing, and, most important for the sake of our story, their music. For the majority of these newcomers, that music was polka. (Believe it or not, you can hear the roots of polka in compositions from eighteenth-century classical composers like Frederic Chopin and Sergei Rachmaninoff.) All of which is why polka has been a major part of my life since I was a kid—it was always there. I guess you could say it was my first love.

But I wasn't alone. If you lived in Florida, you had polka in your blood because the music was everywhere you turned. On the radio: polka. At the high school dances: polka. At weddings: polka. At all the town celebrations: polka. It was all polka all the time, and it was glorious. The bubbly, effervescent melodies . . . the party-inducing beats . . . the lyrics that made you smile, even if they were in Polish and you didn't understand them. I believe that polka was (and is) the reason that Florida was (and is) one heck of a happy town. This isn't to say that there wasn't any other music floating around—I enjoyed Elvis Presley, Jerry Lee Lewis, the Everly Brothers, Gene Vincent, and the like, certainly—but polka was my rock and roll. Why? Because of how it *felt*.

Polka is unlike any other style of music for a variety of reasons, the most notable being its time signature. For you nonmusicians out there, a time signature denotes how many beats there are in a single measure. (To break it down even further, a measure, when you're reading music, is the way a song is subdivided. If that's confusing, it's probably time to go visit your elementary school music teacher.) Most songs sport a 4/4 time signature, meaning there are four beats in a measure subdivided by four. A waltz, on the other hand, is 3/4, meaning three beats in a measure subdivided by four. In rock, soul, classical, and country, 4/4 is the most common time signature, but musicians can use any kind of signature they desire. However, if you're writing or arranging something for a polka band—a *real* polka band—the majority of the time, it'll be in 2/4, although my Orchestra has been known to play a waltz or three. Not only that but the vast majority of polka tunes are formatted in four-measure increments. In other words, all the sections of the song are either four measures long, or eight, or sixteen, or thirty-two, etc. Why all the fours? Because they offer the perfect blueprint for dancing the perfect polka. (You didn't think you'd be getting a musicology lesson from me, did ya?)

When the polka first came to America, its scene, such as it was, became splintered because like all the other European transplants, the practitioners from the different countries in Europe settled all throughout the states. Some planted roots in the New York City area, some around Chicago, and some around Detroit. For example, there were heavy pockets of Slovenians in Pittsburgh and Cleveland, while a good number of Germans settled in Minnesota and Iowa. A huge Polish contingent settled in Buffalo, New York, and they all brought their distinct, individualistic brand of polka to their new homes.

The Slovenian bands, for instance, were mostly small, intimate ensembles, with only an accordion, a bass, drums, sometimes a banjo, and a tenor saxophone. Polish bands, on the other hand, featured two trumpets, three saxophonists, an accordion, and a traditional piano/bass/drums rhythm section. The energetic, driving Polish sound dominated the East Coast, and that was what I grew up listening to; naturally, when it came time to put my band together, that was where I gravitated.

Some of my biggest influences came from the New England area, and the majority of them were of Polish descent. Frank Wojnarowski, for instance, was a native of Sanok, Poland. The Connecticut-based violinist/vocalist had a couple of notable hits, the biggest ones being "Matka (Mother's Waltz)," "Goral," "Jasiu, Jasiu," "Rozmaria," and a cover of "Oh, Suzanna." Gene Wisniewski, whom we'll be discussing in more detail later in this book, was a first-generation American, also based in Connecticut, best known for a nice little ditty called "Open the Door Polka." Walt Solek, another East Coaster, liberally sprinkled comedy into his recordings and was known as "The Polish Spike Jones." Like the aforementioned Mr. Wisniewski, I'll have much more to say about Walt. There was also Bernie Witkowski, a terrific clarinetist from New York City who eventually shared concert bills with the likes of Frank Sinatra, Sophie Tucker, Milton Berle, Jackie Gleason, Xavier Cugat, Benny Goodman, Sammy Kaye, and Harry James.

Al Soyka, who went on to play a key role in my development as a professional musician, had a huge hit with the tune "Trip to Poland." Finally, there was Ray Henry, another Connecticut musician, who was almost as prolific as yours truly, cutting more than eighty records. And, of course, there were the Connecticut Twins, the brothers Stash and Jas, all the way from Bristol, Connecticut.

But that was just the Northeastern polka contingency. In Cleveland, you had Ray Budzilek; in Pennsylvania, you had Joe Resetar and Joe Timmer; and in Massachusetts, you had Larry Chesky, and so on and so on and so on. (If you were to ask me my favorite band, I'd be hard-pressed to give you an answer, because I like them all, but there was one artist who always stood out to me, a man from Waterbury, Connecticut, named Joe Rock. Joe fronted one of those Polish-style bands I loved so much, a ten-piece orchestra that, unlike every other polka band I'd seen, included a trombone player; if you ever want to make people smile, hire a trombone player. Watching someone move his arms like that always gets people laughing.)

These are the men I heard on the radio while I was growing up in Florida, and I listened to the radio *constantly*. My usual system for listening was to press my ear right up against the speaker because oftentimes there was more static than music, as the radio stations were so far away. On Sunday mornings, for example, I'd listen to a station from Connecticut; then in the afternoon, it would be a station from New Jersey. My mother always scolded me when she caught me pressed against the speaker. I can still hear her yelling, "James Sturr Jr., you're gonna go deaf if you keep doing that!" When the static finally drowned out the music, I'd imagine the beats were actually thumping through our radio, filling our living room with those European-tinged, accordion-drenched melodies. I also never missed our local Saturday night polka show.

Since the radio wasn't as consistent as I would've liked, I saved up my allowance and bought every polka record I could get my hands on, a habit that continues to this day; as of this writing, I have more than twelve thousand polka LPs, and close to thirty-five hundred polka CDs down in my basement. And believe it or not, I still have room down there for a radio studio.

At that point, most of my favorite polka artists recorded for a label out of New York City called Dana Records. Dana was founded in 1946 by Walter Dana (his birth name was Wladyslaw Dan Danilowski), and, within a couple of years, it became *the* polka label. If you played a mean polka, you were on Dana. It had 120 or so albums in its catalog, all of which sold and sold and sold. In 1952, *Billboard* noted that Dana was the third-best-selling label in the country, just behind majors like Columbia and RCA Victor, and ahead of Decca, Capitol, and Mercury.

(While polka was an important part of Florida life, some of my friends and family found my rabid interest in the music a bit odd, mostly because the music is associated with Poland, and I'm Irish. When my band began touring and recording regularly, one of the constant refrains from polka purists was, "Don't record Jimmy Sturr, don't produce Jimmy Sturr, don't promote Jimmy Sturr, and don't book Jimmy Sturr. He's not Polish. He's not one of *us*." One of the area Polish newspapers even ran multiple articles about how I was killing polka. I've never understood that; I would've thought their reaction would have been one of ecstasy. First of all, the polka community, while large and fanatical, could always use another warm body out there, keeping the music alive, so it was silly to alienate somebody who was performing and recording the music the right way. Second of all, shouldn't they have been excited that a non-Pole should devote his life to Polish music? It baffled me then and it baffles me now.)

Now don't get me wrong—I didn't obsess about polka all day,

every day, though up to this point it may sound like it. I listened to my fair share of rock and roll, and, as noted, I had other interests, the main one being baseball. I played in the Babe Ruth and American Legion Leagues and was primarily a pitcher, though I sometimes covered first base. After a rainout one Sunday, one of my friends grabbed me by my elbow, pulled me toward his car, and said, "Come on. We're going to a picnic."

I pointed to the gray, waterlogged sky. "But it's raining and it doesn't look like it'll be stopping anytime soon."

"Nah, it'll stop," he said. "Besides, we're going to New Jersey. It never rains in New Jersey."

"What's in New Jersey?" I wondered.

"The guys at the Polish meat market in the center of Florida are having their employee picnic," he explained, "in a town called Oak Ridge."

There wasn't anything else going on, so I said, "Sounds good," and off we went.

I didn't have any expectations, but if I did, this picnic would've exceeded them, no matter how lofty they might have been. I was in awe of the colorful people, the diverse, plentiful food, and, most important, the music. It was the real deal, the Polish brand of polka I'd been hearing for years on the radio, brought to life by local polka heavyweights like Johnny Bud and Frankie Gutowski. Best of all, I didn't have to strain to hear the music over any radio static!

The next week, after our baseball game, my friend told me that there was another one of those picnics out in Jersey, so I hopped into his car and we drove over the border for more food and fun. The following week, and the week after that, same thing. This went on for a while, and it got to the point where I skipped the game and went right to the picnic. For the first time in my life, polka completely trumped sports.

3

A Yankees Interlude

nd while we're on the subject of sports . . .

When he was a young boy, my father worked for a pheasant hunting club. How, you may ask, does a pheasant hunting club work? Well, it's pretty simple: The staff of the club would stock the large wooded area across the valley from our house with pheasants, and the club's clientele would come by with their guns, pay their entry fee, then load up their weapons and shoot themselves a few birds.

My father was a teenager, and they weren't about to let him near any guns, so his primary job was to let the pheasants out of their cages. (In retrospect, one has to wonder if it was such a good idea to have a child in charge of wild birds, but times were different then.) One gray, rainy afternoon, one of the pheasants left his cage, spun around, and headed right toward my father. And that bird was apparently moving *fast*.

In what had to be an instinctual move, one of the adults shot the pheasant right in its side, in an attempt to save my father from a bird attack. That was the good news. The bad news was that this portly man wasn't the best shot in the world. He wasn't even the best shot in Florida. In fact, he also managed to clip my father in the hand.

This portly man's name was George Herman "Babe" Ruth. You'd think that the guy would have better aim, since he could hit and pitch a baseball like nobody's business. Being that it was

Babe Ruth, there was always the possibility he was schnockered. At any rate, I still have the pellet that the doctors removed from my dad's palm. I have to think that's worth something to a collector out there.

This is part of the reason why, as a child, I was a rabid New York Yankees fan and worshipped the likes of such pitchers as Eddie Lopat, Allie Reynolds, and Vic Raschi. (That was one hell of a pitching staff they had back then, believe me. Between 1949 and 1953, they anchored what I'd argue was one of the great starting rotations in Major League Baseball history.) Lopat was a particular favorite, because, like me, he was a lefty; we lefties always have to stick together.

Many, many decades later, my band was playing a show at Carnegie Hall. Before we took the stage, one of my roadies jogged over and breathlessly said, "There's a guy in the audience who used to play for the Yankees!"

I was always up for meeting a professional athlete, especially one who played for my favorite team. "Find out what his name is," I said.

A few minutes later, the roadie jogged on back and huffed, "Eddie Lopat. He says his name is Eddie Lopat."

I put down my sax, looked that roadie dead in the eye, and told him, "Some way, somehow, you make sure that guy gets backstage after the show. He's my idol."

When we finished up the show, I walked toward the stage wings, and standing there, right by the side of the curtain, sure enough, it's Eddie Lopat himself. He was hale and hearty, and looked like he could throw a five-hit shutout against any Major League team right then and there.

Eddie and I got to talking, and it turned out that he was a big hunting and fishing guy. Not only that but thanks to some invites from yours truly, he went to the very same pheasant club where Babe Ruth shot my father. (I should mention that my dad was the club's president. He stayed with them all those years; I suspect that not too many people would have hung around after they got plugged in the hand, but that was my father for you.) Eddie lived in New Jersey, and since that wasn't too far from us, he started making regular trips to the club. He eventually became great friends with my father, which if you look at it a certain way, is kind of poetic justice: a Yankee great befriending a guy who was shot by a great Yankee.

But I digress. Let's get back to the music.

4

Sturr-ing It Up
in the Studio

By the time I was fifteen, I decided that I was ready to cut my first record. Using my father's many professional connections, we got in touch with one Eric Bernet, a gentleman who we were told could point me in the right direction.

Eric was a music industry lifer who owned a "one-stop" in New York City called A-1 Records. (A one-stop is a company where independent record stores can order albums from different labels and distributors, both large and small. Since the music industry has changed so much, one-stops have gone the way of the cassette tape, but back then they were crucial for the tiny mom-and-pop shops that weren't able to establish a line of credit with the major record labels.) One sunny summer Saturday morning, one of my bandmates and I hopped a bus to Manhattan and made our way over to Tenth Avenue to meet with Eric, who proceeded to do everything in his power to convince me it would be in my best interest not to make a record.

"It doesn't make sense for you," he said.

"But—"

"You're too young, you're too inexperienced."

"But I—"

"You're not ready yet."

"Um—"

"There's a lot of competition out there, Jimmy, a lot of competition."

"Er—"

"Lots of great musicians making lots of great music, and they all have a helluva lot more experience than you."

This went on for about forty-five minutes, Eric telling me about my shortcomings, and me not being able to get a word in edgewise. My pervading thought was, *Right now, I could be playing baseball.*

Finally—*finally*—Eric paused, then gave us a considering look and said, "Boys, I want to take you down to my basement."

I was hesitant, because what with the intense way he was talking to me, I wouldn't have been surprised if he would've held me captive. "Why?" I asked.

"I just wanna show you something. Come on. It won't hurt, I promise."

We wound our way through his massive stockroom—it was like a hedge maze, except with records rather than evergreen bushes—then went down a thin, dark, dank stairwell. He turned on the light, and we were greeted by the sight of dusty boxes filled with, you guessed it, more records. "Look at this, kid. Ten thousand jazz records. Some of 'em have been here for months. Some of 'em have been here for years. I can't give 'em away."

"I want to record polka."

Eric scratched his head and gave me a funny look. "*Polka?* Don't you lead a jazz group?"

"Oh no, we're polka."

He grinned like a madman and said, "Ahhhhhhhh, polka! I thought you were a jazz guy. That changes things. Can you be ready to record something this Friday night?"

"Um, s-s-s-s-sure."

Patting me on the shoulder, he said, "Great. At 7 p.m., be at this studio called Gotham Records." He gave me the address and sent me on my merry way.

The following Friday, Florida's finest, Jimmy Sturr and the Golden Bells Orchestra, trekked from the Big Onion to the Big Apple, ready and willing to cut our first single. After we recorded that one song, Eric pulled me aside and breathlessly asked, "Jimmy, kid, d'you have enough material to record an entire album?"

"Yes."

He wiped some sweat from his upper lip and said, "Oh thank God. Let's get to work."

The next track we recorded was an original song of ours, a peppy instrumental called "Hepsa." (Why it was called "Hepsa," I have no clue.) We followed that up with another instrumental called "Sax Polka," after which I laid down a few vocal tracks. It apparently went well, because after our seventh song, Eric poked his head out of the control room and said, "Okay, guys, we need more music from you . . . a *lot* more music. So one week from tonight, I need you at Beltone Studios on Thirty-First Street. Seven o'clock, sharp."

Eric seemed especially excited when he mentioned the name of the studio, so I asked, "What's so special about this Beltone place?"

"What's special about Beltone? *What's special about Beltone?!* Not much . . . except Buddy Holly recorded there, and so did Miles Davis and James Brown and Thelonious Monk. And pretty soon, Jimmy Sturr and the Golden Bells Orchestra!"

That sounded pretty darn good to us. Who were we to refuse?

So at 6:59 p.m. the next Friday, Eric was waiting for us at Beltone's front door. He said, "Thanks for showing up on time, guys. But I have some bad news."

All the blood drained from my face and went straight to my stomach. I thought, *Did we come all the way down here for nothing? Is my chance to record at this hallowed ground out the window?* I steeled myself and asked Eric, "What's up?"

"Johnny Tillotson's session is running late. You guys'll have to wait a few minutes."

Johnny Tillotson was big time, a singer/songwriter whom you could call the Kenny Chesney of his day, a country-tinged artist who found his greatest successes when he sprinkled a bit of pop music into his tunes. I was familiar with a couple of his earlier hits, specifically "Poetry in Motion" and "It Keeps Right On A-Hurtin'," and I certainly appreciated his talent and his sales figures, which is why I had no problem whatsoever cooling my heels while he finished up.

Some forty-five minutes later, after Tillotson called it a night, we took to the studio and set up our equipment. The studio was exceptional on every level: great sound, comfortable atmosphere, and as clean as a whistle. Little wonder that it played home to all those great recordings. After a quick, efficient soundcheck, we cut a track called "Blue Skirt Waltz," a polka favorite that was most memorably performed by Frank Yankovic and His Yanks, a version that sold more than a million copies. Before the final note died, Eric burst into the recording room and roared, "Guys, that was smashing, just smashing! Sounds like you've been doing it for decades. So let me ask you this: What label do you guys want this little gem to come out on? Capitol? Mercury? Roulette? Vee-Jay?"

As we packed up our instruments and cleared out space for the group that had been waiting patiently in the hallway for us to finish, I said, "Mr. Bernet, you tell me. You're the expert. I don't care. I'd be thrilled with any of 'em. We'll go with whomever you think would give us the best opportunity to be heard."

Without hesitation he said, "Vee-Jay." He went on to explain that Vee-Jay was an up-and-coming independent label launched by Vivian Carter (she was the "Vee") and James C. Bracken (he was the "Jay"), a husband-and-wife team from Gary, Indiana. They were best known for recording blues greats such as John Lee Hooker, Memphis Slim, Jimmy Reed, and soul acts like The Spaniels, the Dells, and the El Dorados.

"Do they have any polka acts?" I asked.

"Nah, but that doesn't matter. They know how to break a record, no matter what the style is. Besides, you want go with them, because they're the smallest. You go with a Mercury or a Capitol, yeah, you'll have a big, fancy name to put on your résumé, but I guarantee you'll get lost in the pile. Vee-Jay'll take care of you."

"Sounds great, Mr. Bernet! And I want to thank you from the bottom of my—"

Before I could wrap up my thank-you speech, four strikingly good-looking, noticeably cool young men sauntered into the recording room. Eric pointed to the quartet and said, "If it's okay with you, Jimmy, I'm gonna have these cats lay down some background vocals with you. They're terrific; you'll love 'em. And you should get to know them anyhow, because they're gonna be your labelmates. They're already on Vee-Jay and are having the time of their lives."

I peered at the leader. He was as handsome and charismatic as he could be. If he was even the tiniest bit talented, I figured he'd have it made. "What's the group called?"

"The Four Seasons." He pointed to the leader and said, "That guy over there, the short one, he's called Frankie Valli. I think the world'll be hearing from these guys pretty soon. They're just getting started, so having them on this nice little record of yours will be a good notch in their belt."

Without his experience in the studio with me, who knows where Frankie would've ended up?

Turned out Eric Bernet knew what he was talking about: Vee-Jay was a pretty good place to be. In addition to Frankie Valli and Jimmy Sturr, Vee-Jay put out a couple of records by a little group from England you might've heard of called The Beatles. That was some great company to be in. My recording career was off to a flying start.

Postscript #1: *Soon after our recording session, both Vee-Jay Records and Beltone Studios went bankrupt, and in the process, they lost track of much of their respective property. To this day, the master tapes of my first single for a nationally recognized record label are nowhere to be found. They might've been misplaced, they might've been lost in a fire, or they might be in a museum in suburban Warsaw—who knows. The whole thing is simply heartbreaking.*

Postscript #2: *In the summer of 2007, I trekked out to Atlantic City, New Jersey, to see my former background vocalist Frankie Valli. After the show, I managed to get backstage and land an audience with the man himself. After introducing myself, I said, "You won't remember me, but you laid down some background vocals for me back at Beltone Studios."*

Frankie smiled and said, "You were Bernet's pal! The polka kid. Man, I remember that."

5

Book It!

tylistically speaking, polka was number one in my heart and soul, but country music was a close second. When I was fifteen, in 1956, one of my favorite country artists was Hank Snow. Hank recorded for RCA Victor (with my experience in the music industry, I'd start to become rather business savvy and paid attention to things like what label played home to my preferred artists), and between 1949 and 1965, a whopping thirty-one of his singles made it into the top ten, singles such as "Let Me Go, Lover!" "I'm Moving On," "The Golden Rocket," and "I Don't Hurt Anymore." Whenever I heard one of Hank's songs on the radio—and considering how much those things sold, he was on the radio a lot—I'd think, *How am I ever going to see Hank Snow in person? Guys like him don't get up to the Northeast, and I don't get up to his birthplace in Canada, or his hometown of Nashville. Hmmm . . .*

One afternoon, I was reading some music magazine, and tucked there in the back of the magazine was a little article about Hank and his agent. After I read it several times, an idea started forming that would either lead to something brilliant or something silly.

After some intrepid research, I managed to track down the phone number for Moeller Talent, the company Hank's agent worked for in Nashville. When I finally got the guy on the phone, I said, without much in the way of preamble, "I wanna book Hank Snow for a show. How much would that run me?"

Without hesitation the agent asked, "Where're you located?"

"Just outside of New York City." Okay, maybe I was stretching it with the "just outside" part. As previously mentioned, without traffic, Florida is just under two hours away from Manhattan. With traffic, it could be days.

My voice must've cracked on that one, because the agent asked, "Hey, how old are you?"

Ignoring the question, I again asked, "How much would it be to book Mr. Snow?"

He paused, then said, "Fifteen hundred dollars. Half up front, half after the show."

"Wow. Fifteen hundred bucks? Um, wow."

"How old are you?" the agent repeated.

I wished my voice would hurry up and change into its lower register right then and there. "It doesn't matter. I, um, I have to check with my associates about the feasibility of bringing Hank Snow up to my area. I'll get back to you as soon as I meet with my team."

After I said good-bye and hung up, the wheels started turning . . . and turning . . . and turning. It finally hit me. My band performed regularly at this place in Middletown, New York, called the Orange County Fair. (Middletown is just a hop, skip, and a jump from Florida.) I called up Al Howard, the Orange County Fair's general manager, and said, "Mr. Howard, I have a question for you. How do you feel about Hank Snow?"

"How do I feel about Hank Snow?" he said. "Jimmy, I *love* Hank Snow. The guy is one helluva singer."

"He sure is," I agreed. "And you know what? I think can get him to play at your place."

"What do you mean?" He sounded a bit taken aback. But if some fifteen-year-old pisher told you he could book one of the day's most popular country singers, you'd probably sound a bit taken aback too.

"I talked to his agent, and if some things fall into place, I can get him up here. Is there a way I can use your—"

Without letting me complete my request, Al said, "I'll give you the grandstands for free. I'll take all the money for the food and drinks, and you can have the ticket sales."

It couldn't be that easy, could it? "Really?" I asked.

"Really."

"*Done!*" I hung up, then went over to my father and said, "Dad, I need a favor."

Without taking his nose from his newspaper, he said, "What kind of favor?"

"It's kind of a big one."

The newspaper stayed put. "Do tell."

"I need $750."

Down went the newspaper. "What does a fifteen-year-old need $750 for?"

I gave him a huge grin and said, "I'm booking Hank Snow to play at the Orange County Fairgrounds."

Dad stared at me for a bit, then said, "You're kidding."

"I'm not. He needs half up front. And Mr. Howard and I worked out a deal so I'll make a nice profit on top of it."

He gave me a long, appraising look, then said, "Whom do I make the check out to?"

I called Hank's agent and told him we were a go. Again he asked how old I was, and again I didn't answer.

The contract showed up in the mail a few days later, which I signed and returned to Moeller Talent, with my dad's $750 check enclosed. Just like that, I was a concert promoter.

A couple months later, on a warm Friday evening, Hank

Snow's giant tour bus pulled up to an almost-sold-out Orange County Fairgrounds. I very badly wanted to meet Hank, so as soon as his driver cut the engine, I sauntered up to the door and gave it a tentative knock. A grizzled-looking gentleman poked his head out and asked, "Can I help you, son?"

"Um, yeah. Hi, I'm, um, Jimmy Sturr. Is, um, is there any chance I can, um, meet Mr. Snow?"

"You're Jimmy Sturr?"

"Um, yeah."

"*You?*"

"Um, yeah."

"You're the guy who booked us?"

"Um, yeah."

He gave me a big smile and said, "You bet you can meet Hank!" Then he turned around and called, "Hey, Hank! Jimmy Sturr's here to see you!"

"The man who booked us?" Hank yelled.

The grizzled-looking guy said, "More like the *boy* who booked us."

Hank ambled down through the bus and peered at me for what seemed like ten minutes before asking, "You're Jimmy Sturr?"

"Um, yeah."

"The guy who booked us?"

"Um, yeah."

Nodding, he said, "I'd like to meet your father. I always like to meet the promoter." He squinted, then asked, "Because you're Jimmy Sturr Jr., right? There's no way you could've done this. You're just a kid." He stepped out of the bus and gazed around the grounds. "Where's this Jimmy Sturr Sr. character at?"

I said, "Jimmy Sturr Sr. is at home. I'm Jimmy Sturr Jr., but I'm also just plain Jimmy Sturr. Honest to goodness, I'm the promoter." I pulled the check from my back pocket. "And after the show, I'll be giving you this!"

He chuckled and said, "Well, all right, that's what I like to hear. Come on aboard, son."

After I climbed up the stairs into the bus, Hank sat down next to a tall blonde woman. Like a dummy, I asked him, "Is this your wife, Mr. Snow?"

He snapped, "No, sir, it's not!"

The rest of Hank's band cracked up, and I took that as my cue to leave. I found out later on that evening that the tall blonde was a prostitute Hank had imported from Hartford, Connecticut, just for the show. I realized then and there that I was going to learn some life lessons as a concert promoter.

Like the true professional that he was, Hank took the stage right on time, and played hit after hit after hit: "The Rhumba Boogie," "The Gold Rush Is Over," "Lady's Man," "Spanish Fireball," and "Tangled Mind." He was in great form throughout, and the crowd ate it up. Heck, *I* ate it up. It jazzed me knowing that if it weren't for me, none of these people would be congregated here tonight. The fans would've been in their respective homes, the ticket takers would've had the night off, Hank would still be in Nashville, and the hooker would still be in Hartford. Single-handedly, I changed the lives of all these fine folks, and it felt great.

After the show, and after I bid Hank a fond farewell, I jogged over to the box office where I was handed an envelope . . . a bulging envelope . . . an envelope filled with cash. Lots and lots of cash.

I couldn't wait until I got home to tally up the money, so I found a quiet corner and did some mental bookkeeping. First I pulled out the $750 that was set aside to cover Hank's cut, and then I counted. And counted. And counted. And counted some more.

Double-, triple-, and quadruple-checking the numbers told me that I had made a profit of $3,315. As I got ready to head home, I thought, "Man, this is the job is for me!"

Naturally, the concert booking continued. First there was Hank Thompson and The Brazos Valley Boys (a superb country-western crooner, Hank was the basis for Jeff Bridges' character in the film *Crazy Heart*), then Tom T. Hall of "Harper Valley PTA" fame, then a young Tanya Tucker, then a yet-to-be-famous (and yet-to-be-unhinged) Hank Williams Jr., then future Country Music Hall of Fame inductee Porter Wagoner, then Johnny Cash's brother Tommy, then the legendary "Whispering" Bill Anderson, who eventually became one of my most cherished friends and musical associates.

This was another possible profession in my growing list of possible professions—musician, professional baseball player, and now booking agent. The future was looking bright.

Unfortunately for me and the music fans of Florida, New York, the future was about to be put on hold.

6

Military Man

ince I started school at an early age, I graduated from high school at sixteen, an accomplishment of which I'm still quite proud. In hindsight, however, I kind of wish I'd have taken my time, because during part of my senior year in high school, I was only fifteen. Yes, I was relatively mature—none of my classmates were leading bands, doing recording sessions, booking shows, and playing baseball at a relatively high level— but it might have been better for me had I had the opportunity to hang out with kids who were my own age.

After graduating high school, I received a full scholarship to Valley Forge Military Academy & College in Wayne, Pennsylvania. VFMA&C was founded in 1928 by one Lieutenant General Milton Baker. Baker was an Anglophile and Revolutionary War buff, so many of school's trappings were straight out of 1776. His administration also had an affinity for West Point—if you ran a military academy in the Northeast, you'd *better* have an affinity for West Point, if you knew what was good for you—so our insignia and uniforms were a blend of British-ness and New York-ness. It was different than anything I'd ever experienced at the S.S. Seward Institute, that's for certain.

I wasn't in love with the place, but I sucked it up, in part because I wanted to do right by my parents, and in part because I was getting my education for free, thanks to the music scholarship I'd managed to earn. Having a music scholarship in my back

pocket meant that, in addition to learning how to be a good sol-
dier, I was able to play in both the school band and the marching
band. What I *didn't* play, however, was sports. VFMA&C made
a musical investment in me, and if I hurt myself in an intramural
baseball or football game, the school wouldn't have gotten any
return in this investment, and my scholarship would've gone
down the drain. But that didn't stop me from messing around on
various athletic fields with my classmates. I've always had some
kind of sports in my life—even today I'm in a local Florida tennis
league and play two, three, or sometimes four days a week—and
I wasn't about to stop then.

Going to VFMA&C was, to that point, the hardest thing I'd
ever done in my life. For a kid who'd lived in his small-town
home his entire life and had done nothing but lead a band, play
sports, goof around on snowmobiles, and sneak away to listen to
polka at picnics, well, this was some serious culture shock. The
people were different, the disciplines were different, the goals
were different, the food was different—*everything* was different.
The worst aspect about the whole thing was the rigid regimenta-
tion; we awoke at the crack of dawn, lights out was at 10 p.m.,
and everything in between was timed to a T.

My first year, which is called the plebe year, was particularly
brutal. Aside from the difficulty of the classes, I had to deal with
homesickness (other than my trips home at Christmas and Easter,
I wasn't allowed to leave the campus), constant hazing from the
upperclassmen, and constant verbal abuse from the officers. It
wasn't as bad as standard basic training, but it was darn close.

I didn't agree with some of the school's policies, although I
suspect that every VFMA&C student has had some frustrations
with the teachers or the administration's decisions at one point or
another. At that time, for instance, your rank was determined by
how much money your parents had. Since I'd been a jock in high

school, I was in good shape, so based on that, you'd think that I'd be able to climb through the hierarchy quickly and easily. Well, when I returned for my sophomore year, I was made a non-com, which was a sergeant. However, many of that year's incoming plebes—kids who were supposed to be below me on the totem pole—were ranked higher than me despite the fact that I had a full year's experience on them. But these highly ranked plebes were highly ranked because their parents donated a whole lot of cash to VFMA&C. My mother and father didn't do that. Mind you, I didn't want them to pay for my promotions. If I was going to succeed, I was going to do it the honorable way.

The musical aspect of school wasn't always particularly fulfilling, but that wasn't a shock because I knew going in that VFMA&C wasn't exactly Juilliard. The one good thing about the whole deal was that we played a whole lot of music, all day, every day; the symphonic band plowed through some interesting marches for the appreciative cadets, and our marching band was actually very good. There were even some moments that could actually be called fun. For instance, we performed at a couple of huge parades in the Philadelphia area; when I was an upperclassman, we did a few overseas concerts in England. But there sure as hell wasn't any polka going on.

Or was there?

VFMA&C students had two choices as to how we could spend our Sunday mornings: We could either go to the school's chapel for services, or we could wake up really, really, really early and go up to the nondenominational service at the Catholic Church in nearby Wayne, Pennsylvania. (If you went to Wayne, you were exempt from chapel.) I opted for the early-bird special, as did some of the Catholic guys in the band. When we'd return to the barracks, we'd go off to the band room and play some polkas.

One Sunday afternoon, an English gentleman named Colonel

Mulhart, who was considered the toughest of our tough teachers, burst into the room and roared, "What the hell is that racket you guys are playing?"

I said, "Polkas, sir."

"What the hell is a polka?" I launched into a thumbnail sketch of the music, but he cut me off pretty quickly. "I don't really care and I don't like it one bit. If you keep playing this junk, you'll never amount to anything." After about ten more minutes of yelling at us, he stomped off. Fortunately, he didn't bring us up on charges; he probably realized that we couldn't be court-martialed for playing European dance music.

All of this hell was worth it. VFMA&C was a daily struggle; when I went into the army a couple of years later, I won every award that could be won because I'd already learned and perfected everything I needed to know to be a good military man. And those awards weren't only ego boosters; each win earned me a forty-eight-hour furlough. Whenever I got my two-day pass out of Fort Dix, I'd make my way from Trenton, New Jersey, back to Florida, and play in as many polka jam sessions or softball games as I possibly could.

Postscript: *Several decades later, after I took home what I believe was my tenth Grammy Award, VFMA&C honored me as its Man of the Year, something that I still consider to be one of the greatest honors of my life. Before I gave my thank-you speech, I peered out into the audience, and who's sitting right there in the front row? None other than my polka-hating nemesis, Colonel Mulhart. Our eyes met, and he gave me a friendly nod. As I nodded back, I thought, I'll never amount to anything playing that crap? Every cadet at the school is here in full dress, all because of polka music. Take that, you sonofabitch!*

Jimmy receiving the Man of the Year award at his alma mater, Valley Forge Military Academy & College.

7

Radio Days, Part One

After graduating from Valley Forge Military Academy & College, I used all of that hard-core military training not to build a bomb or take over Belgium, but to land a job at an insurance company called Dickerson & Meany in Goshen, New York. The primary reason I landed the job wasn't because of the skills I'd picked up at VFMA&C, but rather because the Meany half of Dickerson & Meany was one of my father's best friends.

Initially, working as an insurance agent was a comedown, to say the least. Think about it. In high school, in addition to recording and performing with my band, I had the opportunity to excel at almost any sport my heart desired. VFMA&C and the army, while difficult and oftentimes depressing, were always, at the very least, interesting. Selling insurance wasn't. I didn't envision myself doing it for a living—for that matter, I could barely envision myself doing it for another week—but I stayed with Dickerson & Meany all the way up until I fulfilled my military duty with the National Guard. Sometimes, as they say, ya gotta do what ya gotta do.

I'd spent two years in the army and four in the National Guard, so it's understandable why, at that point in my life, I couldn't envision making a living playing music. Besides, I didn't even know anybody who was paying their bills with polka, so I was scared to take the plunge. I mean, I was a young kid from a small town; how was I ever going to make a dent in the music world? There were probably so many other musicians who were going for it, what chance did I have of succeeding? Sure, when I was growing up, there were polka concerts all throughout the area, but since most of the shows were at outdoor festivals, it wasn't a year-round thing. For that matter, it wasn't even a half-year-round thing, and I couldn't imagine giving myself any kind of financial cushion making music.

Which brings us to the Onion Harvest Festival.

Since its inception in 1939, every five years Florida plays host to the Onion Harvest Festival. This may sound quaint to you big-city folks, but this thing is *huge*—we're talking as many as fifteen thousand attendees, even back in its earliest days. The reason it is held five years apart is because that's how long it takes to prepare. The Monday after, say, the 1959 festival ended, the committee had to start planning and plotting for 1964.

All that planning and plotting paid off because the festival was, without fail, always quite a spectacle. Aside from having access to all the onions you could ever want, you could enjoy dance troupes that performed traditional Polish dances. Those troupes were composed of up to one-hundred and fifty people of all ages, from kindergarteners to grandparents. I imagine that it took a good portion of those five-year periods to teach these amateur dancers how to move together in lockstep.

In 1961 the two men in charge of the 1964 Onion Harvest Festival, popular local attorney Michael Gurda and Monsignor Felczak, held a planning meeting at Mr. Gurda's house, a meeting to which I was invited. I had no clue why I was asked to join the festivities. Maybe it was because I was a precocious kid who led a band. Maybe it was because my family had known Mr. Gurda for years. Maybe it was because Mr. Gurda made a mistake and invited Jimmy Sturr Jr. rather than Jimmy Sturr Sr. Whatever the

Jimmy in Polish costume leading the band at the 1989 Onion Harvest Festival.

reason, I was one of fifty or so people packed into Mr. Gurda's living room.

Our host was handing out assignments—this person was in charge of bratwurst, that person was in charge of liquid refreshments, this other person was in charge of the first-aid tent—and near the end of the meeting, after reading off another one of his never-ending lists, Mr. Gurda pointed at me said, "And Jimmy Sturr over here and his polka band will be playing at the festival."

"Um, I am?" I asked.

"You are," Mr. Gurda said.

"Are you sure?"

"Very much so."

Hit with a wave of nerves and delight, I could barely speak. This would be by far the biggest show I had ever played, and I was thrilled.

First thing the next morning, I called Mr. Gurda to thank him. "Polka is everything to me," I explained. "I can't believe I get to play for all those people. That's all I want to do—share the music with the world. This is my dream come true." I then joked, "The only thing that could possibly top this is if I had my own weekly radio polka show, but I know that'll never happen. I'm just a kid."

He paused, then said, "Where are you right now?"

"At home."

"I need your phone number." After I gave it to him, he said, "I'll call you back in five minutes. Don't leave your house. Stay by the phone." As instructed, I hovered over the telephone, and, sure enough, he called back five minutes later. "The general manager of WALL-AM in Middletown is waiting to meet with you right now. Go up there and—"

Before he was able to finish the sentence, I yelled, "Thanks a million, Mr. Gurda," and then I slammed down the phone, sprinted out to the car, jammed the key into the ignition, put the pedal to the metal, and headed up to the neighboring town. When I arrived at the station, I was ushered into the station's general manager's office. After we shook hands, he said, "So Mike Gurda tells me you're something of a polka maven . . ."

I felt myself blushing. "I don't know if I'd say *maven*."

"Take a compliment, kid. Mike also told me that you want to host a polka show. When would you want this show to air?"

"How about Sundays? In the afternoon? At one o'clock?" I'm not sure where the day and time came from, but there it was.

Nodding, the general manager said, "When can you start, kid?"

It's a good thing I was sitting down, because a light breeze probably would've knocked me on my butt. "Um, I don't know," I said. "When do you want me to start?"

He made a show of looking at his calendar, then asked, "Can you be ready next Sunday?"

"Um, sure." I should probably mention that I'd never been on the radio, I had no radio training, and, up until that very moment, I had never set foot in a radio station. I'd listened to more than my fair share of radio, of course, so I knew what went into making a show sound good, but I had no clue how to do it.

"You know what you're doing, kid?" the general manager asked.

"I . . . I . . . I . . . I . . ."

"I didn't think so," he said. "But don't worry about it. Just come in every night this week and pay attention to the deejays. You seem like a bright kid. You'll figure it out. See ya tomorrow."

As instructed, the next night, which was a Tuesday, a mere five days away from my big debut, I made the drive to Middletown, parked myself in the studio, and, keeping my mouth shut the entire time, paid close attention to the on-air personalities. I noted how they delivered their in-between-song banter, studied their energy level (sometimes you had to speak emphatically and sometimes you had to keep it relaxed), and discerned how they read the advertisements. On Wednesday they let me say a few things on the air; on Thursday they let me twist and turn some of the dials. Considering my life path, it's more than fair to say that that one week of schooling at WALL was more important than my four years at Valley Forge.

Come Sunday, I thought I was ready to go on the air. The general manager knew better and he wisely had one of his veteran on-air personalities hover over my shoulder for the entire show, making sure I didn't knock us off the air, or blow anything up, or sell us to the Russians. I survived and I must've done okay, because they invited me back the next week . . . and the next week . . . and the week after that.

Since then, I've been on the air on one station or another each and every Sunday. I'm proud to say that in those four-plus decades, I've never missed a single show. Right now, I record my show, which is syndicated nationally, in my basement during the week, but it still airs on Sunday, so my consecutive-game streak remains intact. If you want to put it in baseball terms (an opportunity I rarely pass up), I guess you could say I'm the Cal Ripken Jr. of polka-radio-show hosts, the guy who will keep playing the game week in and week out, until he decides it's time to hang it up.

And I can't imagine ever hanging it up. *Ever.* But there were some sordid events in my early radio days that almost turned me against the medium forever.

8

Radio Days, Part Two

I t was sometime in the late 1970s when a man named Jim O'Grady, one of the nicest guys you'll ever meet, bought WALL-AM. (Fortunately, Jim liked me *and* polka music, so I was kept on the schedule when his regime took over.) A couple of years later, WTBQ-AM, another local radio station in nearby Warwick, New York, went up for sale. I was familiar with WTBQ because it had its own polka show on Saturdays. The show's host, a blowhard named Ron Kurowski, had an unhealthy hatred for yours truly; he despised me as a disc jockey and even more so as a bandleader. Kurowski disliked me so much that he always used a chunk of his weekly airtime to knock me.

"I don't know how many of you listen to that Jimmy Sturr fella over on WALL," Ron would say, "but if you do, you shouldn't! I mean, what's a non-Polish guy doing playing polka on the radio? Jimmy Sturr, stop pulling the wool over the Polish people's eyes! Listeners, if you care about polka music being played by a real polka person, call up WALL, or write them a letter, and demand that they fire that fraud! And, of course, you'd better not buy any of his records, records that you can be sure I'll never play, because Jimmy Sturr is a blight on the polka community!" Wow. Nineteen years old and already a blight.

This went on week in and week out. One day, after a particu-larly personal attack questioning my parentage, I tracked down the owner of WTBQ, a decent fellow named Ed Klein, and told him, "Listen, I don't care if Kurowski doesn't play my records, but you've got to stop him from talking trash about me on the radio. He's embarrassing me, he's embarrassing my family, he's embarrassing the polka community, and, frankly, he's embarrassing himself."

Without hesitation, Ed said, "You got it. No problem."

I listened to the show the next Saturday, and Kurowski didn't mention my name once. The following week, however, he mentioned it a whole bunch. It was the usual litany of how my not being Polish is a black mark on polka, and how I shouldn't be allowed either on the air or in a recording studio, blah, blah, blah, blah, blah. The fact that he disregarded his boss's order put me over the edge.

So first thing on Monday morning, I burst into my lawyer's office and said, "Enough is enough. I've been polite about this business with Kurowski, but I'm done being Mr. Nice Guy. Let's sue this jerk into the next century."

My lawyer said, "It could take years for the case to get settled. Libel is tricky."

"I don't care."

"It might be expensive," he said.

"I don't care," I repeated. "Do it, and do it *now*."

The papers were filed by lunch.

The next day, I got a call at my office from Ed Klein himself.

"Jimmmmmmmmy," he said, trying to be chummy. "Jimmy, Jimmy, Jimmy, kiddo, you didn't have to bring the law into it. We can work something out."

"Mr. Klein," I said, "Kurowski clearly isn't going to listen to you, and I'm fed up with it. Enough is enough. I feel like this is the only way to nip this in the bud."

Ed was quiet for a moment, and then he sighed and said, "Is there anything we can do to make this right for you?"

"You bet there is!"

"And that would be what?"

"Get rid of him. Fire Kurowski, and I'll drop the lawsuit."

"You know what, Jimmy?" Ed said. "I'd do it in a heartbeat, but I don't have anybody to take his place."

I chuckled, then said, "Yes, you do."

"I do?"

"Yeah."

"Who?" he asked.

"Don't worry about it. He's good. He'll be there first thing on Saturday morning."

"Great!" Ed said. "I'll can Kurowski as soon as I hang up here." He paused, then asked, "And you'll drop the suit, right?"

"Consider it dropped."

Sure enough, Ron was out of a job that very day; the following weekend, my great, great friend Gus Koisor was the new Saturday morning polka voice of WTBQ. And Gussie did one hell of a job, believe me. Between Gus on Saturday and me on Sunday, polka fans in the area were set for the weekend.

A few months later, out of nowhere, Ed Klein rang me up. "Jimmy, I just wanted to let you know that WTBQ is going up for sale."

"Wow. That's interesting news. But why are you telling me?"

"Because," Ed said, "you seem to know good people—everybody loves that friend of yours, Gussie—and you seem to be able to make things happen. So I'm thinking you might be able to find a buyer."

I did have an idea for a buyer—me!

Jim O'Grady and I went out for lunch the following day. After a couple of drinks, I launched into my pitch: "Look, Jim, I've been with you for a long time. WALL gave me my first shot on the air and you've always supported me, and I appreciate all of this more than you can ever know. But WTBQ is going up for sale, and—"

He interrupted me. "And you want to go work for them."

"No, Jim," I said. "I want to *buy* them."

Jim threw down the rest of his drink. "So you're gonna be my competition now."

"I don't want to compete with you, Jim," I said. "First of all, we're great friends, and I would never do anything to screw you over. Second of all, I just want all of the listeners out there to have as many options as possible, regardless of the style of music. I want people in Florida and beyond to have the opportunity to listen to *what* they want, *when* they want. I don't want to knock you off the air and I sure hope you won't try to put me out of business."

"Well, I certainly appreciate that," Jim said, smiling. "I'm willing to work together if you are."

"Funny you mention that," I said. "There's one other thing I wanted to float by you."

"What's that?"

"I'd like to keep my Sunday morning show on WALL."

After ordering another drink, he said, "Let me get this straight. You want to own WTBQ, while appearing on WALL at the same time? Do I have that right?"

"You sure do!"

Jim chewed on his thumbnail, then said, "You know what? That's A-OK with me. As long as you don't say anything about WTBQ while you're on the air at WALL, I have no problems."

"Wouldn't even dream of it."

My purchase of WTBQ went through without a hitch, and the

two stations coexisted peacefully for the next couple of years, until Jim sold WALL to the Sillerman-Morrow Broadcasting Group, a newly formed conglomerate fronted by Bob Sillerman and Bruce Morrow that was buying up radio stations left and right.

And from there, it all went downhill at good ol' WALL-AM.

9

Cousin Brucie & Robert F. X.

Being a radio hound, I was well aware of Bruce Morrow, a.k.a. Cousin Brucie. He was, after all, one of the greats.

Bruce Morrow, whose real name is Bruce Meyerowitz, became known to New York City radio listeners in 1959, when he landed a slot playing the hits of the day on WINS. Morrow garnered a solid fan base because he was an excellent disc jockey with terrific taste in music and a nose for what was going to be The Next Big Thing. The following year he moved over to WABC, where he continued to play the top forty, somehow managing to increase his listenership at least tenfold. It might not have been the nicest thing in the world to jump ship from the station that gave you your start to its direct competition, but Cousin Brucie was an ambitious sort. His priorities were what his priorities were, so who was I to argue?

As the decade progressed, Morrow gained even more fans because, unlike the majority of the other jocks out there, he mixed up his playlists, going beyond the top forty and incorporating soul, blues, and R&B. And his WABC show was seamless, so seamless that you almost didn't notice the commercials. Cousin Brucie became so popular that, in 1965, he was tapped to introduce The Beatles at the band's now-revered Shea Stadium concert.

In 1974 Morrow left WABC for *its* chief rival, WNBC, a move that I considered, well, silly. Leaving a good employer in the lurch one time is forgivable, but if you do it twice, well, that's dirty pool, and certainly not the way I work. Cousin Brucie had been with WABC for more than a decade, and while he'd done plenty for its ratings, WABC had done plenty for his career. Sure, something may have gone on behind the scenes that nobody knew about, but from where I was sitting, I thought loyalty should've trumped whatever problems they might have had. At some point during his three-year tenure at WNBC, he crossed paths with Bob Sillerman, and a business marriage was consummated.

Robert F.X. Sillerman (I have no idea what the "F.X." stands for) was a businessman who, as far as I could tell, didn't have much interest in what radio was all about. To me, the purpose of radio was *sharing*, introducing your listeners to music they might have never otherwise heard, or letting them enjoy some of their old favorites. It was, and is, a celebratory medium. My goal, as both a station owner and an on-air personality, was to keep it as pure as possible. To Sillerman, the purpose of radio was to make money. You can't fault the guy for that—there's nothing wrong with wanting to be able to pay your bills and sock something away for your kids, your grandkids, and their kids—but it just wasn't the way I thought.

In 1978, not too long after forming the Sillerman-Morrow Broadcasting Group, Bruce and Robert purchased a slew of radio and television stations, one of which was WALL-AM. Since I owned WTBQ and had no personal connection with Sillerman-Morrow, I figured my Sunday morning polka show was done.

Soon after Jim O'Grady told me about the sale, I got a phone call. "Jimmy Sturr, it's Bruce Morrow."

"Cousin Brucie?"

"One and the same. Listen, I wanna have lunch with you. You wanna have lunch? Let's have lunch. I'll come down to Goshen, and we'll eat something, we'll kibbitz, and we'll have a great time."

We met the next day. Over the biggest salad I've ever seen in my life, Cousin Brucie and I talked shop, trading war stories about hosting a radio show. (Naturally, his stories were far more interesting than mine.) Finally, after about forty-five minutes, he got down to business. "Listen, Jimmy, you and me, we're going to be friendly competitors."

"We are?"

"You bet. As a demonstration of good faith, I'd like you to continue doing your show on WALL. You stay right where you are, right there on Sunday mornings, playing that polka music of yours. I've heard so much about you. I listened to some tapes of the show and I think the world of you. As long as I'm around, you'll always have a home at WALL."

I was shocked. It sounded too good to be true, but as I looked into his eyes, I saw no sign of malice or deceit. But the truth was, he'd have been foolish to let me go because that polka music of mine was WALL's highest-rated show, and he knew it. Cousin Brucie wasn't being either kind or magnanimous. He was being a smart businessman. Naturally, I agreed to stay with WALL, so we parted on a positive note, and I headed home.

The second I walked into the door, the phone rang. It was Jim O'Grady. "Jimmy," he said, "you were just at lunch with Bruce Morrow, weren't you?"

"Yeah. How did you know?"

Ignoring my question, he said, "Don't you believe a word that comes out of Bruce Morrow's mouth."

"What're you talking about?"

He sighed, steeled himself, then said, "This coming Sunday is going to be your last show on WALL."

"But he just told me at lunch—"

"I know what he told you at lunch," Jim said, "but the fact of the matter is that they're going to ambush you. They're going to fire you right after the show on Sunday."

I chuckled, then told Jim, "No, they're not."

"Yeah, they are. I heard it from—"

"Jim, they can't fire me on Sunday, because I'm not going to be at the station. I'm taping the show on Friday, because my band is playing at a telethon in New York on Sunday afternoon."

"Is that the Lions Foundation telethon?" Jim asked.

"Yeah. How did you know about that?"

"Morrow's going to be there, too. He's the emcee."

"You're kidding."

Jim chuckled. "I kind of wish I could be there. Sounds like there could be fireworks."

Fast-forward to Sunday night, the night of the telethon. Cousin Brucie and I didn't see each other until he joined me onstage for the band introduction. After he announced me to the audience, he put his arm around me and said, "Ladies and gentlemen, I'm thrilled to hear what our next group has to offer, because, well, this gentleman right here and I are what you call friendly rivals. I just bought a radio station up in Middletown, and Jimmy here owns the station down the street. And the funny thing is that Jimmy has his own show on my new station! That's not the kind of thing you'd see in New York City, believe you me."

I grinned through his speech . . . or at least I thought I grinned. I was probably actually gritting my teeth, knowing that this guy who was extolling my virtues in front of a rapt audience was getting ready to can me.

What Cousin Brucie didn't know was that when I taped that Sunday's show, in between each song, I roared, "This is my last show on WALL. But make sure that you tune into WTBQ next Sunday at this same time for *The Jimmy Sturr Show*. That's right, each and every Sunday, you can hear *The Jimmy Sturr Show* on WTBQ. Not WALL. WTBQ." I must've said that twenty or thirty times. Loudly.

On Monday morning, I walked into the office and before I could even pour myself a cup of coffee, the phone rang. My secretary picked up on the first ring, then put the caller on hold and told me, "You have a call from Cousin Brucie."

"I bet I do," I said. Then I snatched up the phone and, in my most cheerful voice, said, "The great Bruce Morrow! Good morning! How're you doing on this fine Monday? Hey, I never told you how much fun the boys and I had at the telethon on Saturday. Your introduction was so kind, and—"

"Sturr," he roared, "you &^$@! You don't pull that %@## on me . . . *Nobody* pulls that %@## on me. Don't you know who I am? Don't you know what I've done? I'm an icon, and you're a nobody from nowhere, and I'm gonna do everything in my power to crush you and your pissant station, and your pissant polka, and I'm gonna . . ."

After ten more minutes of yelling, cursing, and threats, he finally ran out of gas. I said, "You done?"

"For now."

I said, "Fantastic. I listened to you, and now you're going to listen to me, Bruce. I may be a country bumpkin, but don't you ever try to pull the wool over my eyes." And then I slammed the phone down as hard as I could. It's a wonder I didn't break the desk.

I think good ol' Cousin Brucie wasn't used to not having the last word because, in a move eerily similar to Ron Kurowski's, he took to bashing me on the air during his afternoon show. "It's your Cousin Brucie here," he'd say, "and I'm sure you can all hear me loud and clear, because we here at WALL-AM, well, we have one heck of a signal, unlike WTBQ's. Ah, yes, WTBQ, Jimmy Sturr's little station that you can't hear unless you're within a three-block radius . . . and that's only if the wind is blowing in the right direction."

I couldn't argue with that. WALL had considerably more juice than we did, and his barbs about our lack of power bothered me for a while . . . until we got the next batch of Nielsen ratings. We weren't number one. We weren't number five. We weren't even number ten. But Jimmy Sturr's WTBQ was well ahead of Bruce Morrow's WALL, and that was good enough for me.

I haven't heard a word from Cousin Brucie since.

Postscript: *Within two years, most every one of WALL's quality employees left Cousin Brucie's House of Horrors and took a job over at the greener pastures of WTBQ. Within five years, the Sillerman-Morrow Broadcasting Group sold WALL.*

And don't forget: Each and every Sunday, if you search around your radio dial, you'll probably stumble across The Jimmy Sturr Show.

Jimmy at the radio controls doing his radio show on WALL Radio. The show, now on WTBQ, started in 1964 and continues every Sunday to this day.

10

If You Want Something Done Right . . .

It always impressed me how the generation of polka musicians who came before me had such an entrepreneurial spirit and how they were able to record and distribute their music when the record company bigwigs wanted nothing to do with them. Comparatively speaking, I was lucky. Without even trying hard, I managed to land a session with Vee-Jay Records, but as I soon learned, that wasn't common. From the late 1930s to the mid-1950s, most major labels and large independents didn't showed much interest in polka, so to get their music out there, these guys had to do it themselves.

Al Soyka was one of the guys who hooked up with a major label (in his case it was RCA). He must've gotten fed up with the whole process because he launched not one but two labels of his own; the first was called Jan Records, and the second, Glo Records. He even managed to have some mainstream success on Glo with one of his own tunes called "Trip to Poland." (I have a special place in my heart for that tune, so much so that I called two of my albums *Trip to Poland* and *Another Trip to Poland*.) To make life easier on himself—and, I suspect, to maintain as much control of his fortunes as possible—most of his sessions were held in his studio in Somers, Connecticut, which was called Main Street. It should be noted that Al built the studio all by himself—in a barn.

A few years after my Vee-Jay adventure, I decided it was time to hit the studio again, so I drove the two-and-a-half hours from Florida to Somers to meet with Al and find out if he'd be interested in getting into the Jimmy Sturr business. Al couldn't have been nicer or more supportive; within ten minutes of my arrival, we'd set up a date to cut my first album for Glo. After we hammered out some of the details, he led me outside and pointed to a gentleman on a ladder, painting his barn/studio.

"See that guy?" he said.

"Yeah. He doesn't look like he's having all that much fun."

"On the contrary," Al said. "He's having the time of his life, because in exchange for all his hard work, I'm giving him a bunch of free studio time."

"Good deal! Is he any good?"

"*Very* good. His name is Gene Pitney. Remember that name. He's going to be big."

Turned out Al was right—Gene Pitney *was* very good, and he did become big. Gene went on to have ten top ten hits, including "Blue Angel," "Twenty-Four Hours from Tulsa," and, most memorably, "(The Man Who Shot) Liberty Valance." In 1964 he played on a record with The Rolling Stones, which means that as a kid, I was only three degrees of separation away from Mick Jagger.

I ultimately recorded five albums in Al's studio (without having to paint the barn), the first of which was cut in 1965. Al went above and beyond for me; not only did he offer my band a chance to record but he also booked us on our first-ever road trip, a series of shows over a long-ago July 4th weekend. For $250, we performed in Boston; Mendon, Massachusetts; and Stafford Springs, Connecticut. Al's band headlined, of course, so it wasn't a particularly glamorous tour for our unit. All eight of us crammed into my father's station wagon; all of our equipment was packed tightly into a U-Haul. Believe me, these days, whenever my band is traveling in our comfortable tour bus, I think about that weekend and count my blessings.

We sold my Glo Records albums at shows, at festivals, and through the mail, but mostly at record shops that we referred to as "mom-and-pop stores." (Among my favorites mom-and-pops: Buffalo, New York's Ruda Records, Johnny Stavin's Records in Elizabeth, New Jersey, and Zack Music right in the heart of my beloved Florida.) The particular mom-and-pops sold nothing but polka records and had everybody's work—hard-to-find stuff from heroes of mine like Frank Wojnarowski, Gene Wisniewski, Bernie Witkowski, Ray Henry, Ray Budzilek, Joe Resetar, and Larry Chesky, as well as other luminaries like Johnny Pecon, Wally Jagiello, Eddie Zima, Marion Lush, Mattie Madura, Dick Pillar, Marisha Data, Harold Loeffelmacher, Steve Adamczyk, Dick Rogers, "Whoopee John" Wilfahrt, Brunon Kryger, and Marv Herzog, to name a few. Today, a mom-and-pop place couldn't survive selling only one genre, especially a genre like polka, which, while still a more-than-viable entity, doesn't carry the same weight as it did in the good old days. But back in the late sixties and seventies, the polka fan base was so rabid, loyal, and insatiable that there was room all across the country for polka-only shops.

In the midst of one of our Northeastern tours, I got a call from a producer at a label called Dyno Records out of Pittsburgh. I was aware of Dyno—the great Marion Lush put out a whole bunch of sides with them, including *Lush's Luscious Polkas* (one of the finest album titles in polka history)—and was tickled, to put it mildly. The conversation was quick and to the point: "Dyno wants to get into the Jimmy Sturr business. Interested?"

"Um, let me check with my current label."

"Great. Call us back." And that was it. He hung up the phone.

Al Soyka had given me a chance to record in his studio and

tour with his band, so I couldn't just up and leave him. After days of contemplating, hand-wringing, and pacing, I made the call I'd been so dreading.

"Al, it's Jimmy."

"Jimmy, my boy. What's up?"

"Well, this is really hard for me to tell you, because you've been so good to me, both as a mentor and a producer, and the last thing I want is to leave you in the lurch, and this is one of the most difficult phone calls I've ever had to make, and I don't know how to tell you this, but, well, but, um, but I got a call from a gentleman at Dyno R—"

Before I could even finish saying the word "records," Al burst in and said, "They want to record you? Great! Do it. I'm moving to Florida. And not your Florida, Jim. The real Florida. You know, with the sun. So go to Dyno! Have yourself a ball! You have my blessing."

As tough as it was to leave Al, moving to a different label was exciting. I'd get new ideas from new producers, and the label's distribution was somewhat better than Glo's, so I'd hopefully be reaching a wider audience. But it was also nerve-racking, as I wouldn't have the savvy of an expert like Al at my disposal. But you have to grow and evolve, so I went for it.

And I proceeded to make the worst album of my life. I've made 140 albums, so that's saying something. The mix was terrible, the song choices were questionable, and the artwork was shoddy. I don't even want to tell you what it was called because you might track it down, buy it, listen to it, and think less of me. I washed my hands of Dyno as soon as I possibly could.

After that disaster, I found myself at a career crossroads. Al was on his way to Florida—the Florida with the sun—and Dyno was clearly useless. Dana Records wasn't particularly active, and I was pretty certain that there weren't going to be any major labels knocking down my door. I weighed my options and came to the conclusion that if somebody was going to produce, record, and distribute my albums, it should be a guy who loves polka, a guy who will promote the hell out of these songs, and a guy who won't argue with me when I want to record a twenty-song medley. And that person was . . . *me!*

Thus, Starr Records was born.

Since I wasn't rolling in the dough, Starr Records was a bare-bones operation. The office staff consisted of yours truly, Gussie Koisor, and, every once in a while, a secretary. In the beginning, our artist roster was small, young, and hungry; it consisted of yours truly, the excellent Kryger Brothers Orchestra from Wilkes-Barre, Pennsylvania, and the hugely popular Max Smule-wicz & His Orchestra. (Years before, Max was the leader of the aforementioned Gay Musicians.)

And then there were the Merry Cavaliers.

I learned early on that being a music-label maven came with its own problems, one of which was the constant barrage of requests for record contracts. In one particularly memorable instance, I received a phone call from a Walt Dombrowski, who introduced himself as the "Polka King of Philadelphia."

"Ah, your highness," I said, chuckling at his self-proclaimed royalty, "what can I do for you today?"

"I want to meet with you," the king commanded. "How about we get together this afternoon? At the train station. In Newark."

"Um, what?"

"Yeah, I'm on my way up to visit my daughter who lives up in New Haven, Connecticut. Florida's about halfway between here and there. I'll get off the train, we'll talk, and then I'll get on the next one and be on my way."

I didn't have much going on that afternoon, so I told him I'd be there. Besides, who was I to refuse an invitation from the king?

When I arrived at the station, a short, squat, older man carrying what looked like one heck of a heavy suitcase wandered over, gave me a once over, and then said, "Sturr?"

"King?"

Smiling, he said, "You know what, Sturr? Just by looking at you, I can tell you're gonna make it someday. You're gonna make it *big*."

"Thanks, Mr.Dombrowski. That's very kind of you to say."

"Just calling it like I see it. So listen, I'm retiring from the music scene, and I want you to have this," he said, and handed me the suitcase.

"What's this?" I asked, hoping it wasn't a bomb, or a decapitated head. After all, I didn't know if Walt was a benevolent king or an angry one.

Walt said, "They're my arrangements. And now they're yours. I think you'll do the right thing with 'em. There're a few of them in there that haven't even been recorded yet. I put those on top." He checked his watch and then said, "The next train is in a few minutes. Good luck, Jimmy, but I don't think you'll need it." Then he repeated, "I can tell you're gonna make it someday. You're gonna make it *big*."

When I arrived home, I did some research, which consisted of me ringing up one of my polka-loving pals from Pennsylvania, and learned that Walt was kind of a big deal at one time. He'd cut some albums for RCA, and once that well dried up he, like most quality purveyors of polka, moved over to Dana Records. All of a sudden, the king's arrangements started to mean something to me; I wanted to get them on wax ASAP. That weekend I got my band together, and we drove up to West Point, New York. Why would I go to West Point, instead of one of the many established studios in Manhattan? Simple—because one of my oldest and dearest friends was the West Point house engineer, and he was going to give me a good deal. And at that time, Starr Records needed all the good deals it could possibly get.

Unsurprisingly, West Point didn't have the best facilities in the world; the academy was all about building soldiers, not making records. It had only two tracks, and the West Point brass wasn't compelled to update it, because its only client was the school band. As my friend explained, the powers-that-be weren't particularly concerned about the sonics for a band whose records would never sell outside of the campus. But I was getting a bargain, so I'd take what I could get. His name was Bill Turowski. After seven years in the army, he went away to become a priest and eventually became the parish priest in my hometown.

After the session, Gus and I were listening to the master tapes; halfway through the first song, something dawned on me. "You know what?" I said to Gussie. "This doesn't sound like us. Not one bit."

He said, "It's Walt's arrangements. They're great, but they're not you."

"You're right. But you know what? I think the record's pretty good."

"It's not bad," Gus said. "Not bad at all."

"We can't let it sit there just because it sounds a little different. We have to release it."

Scratching his head, Gus suggested, "Why don't you put it out under a different name? Something with 'Bells,' maybe. Everybody still likes that 'Bells' business. You could be the Ringing Bells. Or the Blue Bells, or maybe the New York Bells. Or even the Northern Bells . . ."

"No," I said. "No way. 'Bells' has been done to death. No 'Bells' on Starr Records."

"Got it. How about something with 'Happy'? The Happy Campers. The Happy Orchestra. Happy Bells. The Bells of Happiness."

"Happy's too simple. How about 'Cheerful'?"

"Or 'Jolly'?"

"Or 'Jovial'?"

"Or 'Merry'?"

"Hey, 'Merry' is good."

I'll spare you the discussion that led to us coming up with "Cavaliers."

The debut from the Merry Cavaliers Orchestra was an interesting record (I listened to it not too long ago, and it still sounds pretty good to me); however, from what I understand, the Polka King of Philadelphia passed away before he was able to hear it, which is really too bad. I think he would've enjoyed it.

Another one of the gentlemen I welcomed into the Starr stable was my old favorite Walt Solek. As noted, Walt was a comedic performer, so he was called the "Clown Prince of Polka," thanks in part to his crossover novelty composition "Who Stole the Kishka?" (Walt wasn't just funny in the studio; he also liked to goof around in concert. One of his favorite gags was to take the stage in a striped jailbird costume when he played his big hit. I doubt anybody ever got arrested for stealing a *kishka*, but I could be wrong.) I'd put together some semicomedic arrangements of my own—the most memorable one was called "Plumbers Polka," which included a line about not being able to hold a pipe anymore (you can take that as you will)—and figured a guest appearance from the Clown Prince would put those songs over the top. And since this comedic repertoire didn't sound like my band, it was released under the banner of Walt Solek and the Merry Cavaliers.

While we're on the subject of stealing, I wasn't above stealing from another record label's roster, although this particular theft was instigated by the musician himself.

One day out of the blue, I got a call from Dyno Records recording artist Marion Lush. At this point Marion was one of the most popular artists in the entire polka field, so when he said, "Would you be interested in signing me to Starr Records?" I jumped on it. We released a bunch of Marion's records, including the awkwardly named *For Adults Only Polka Party Album*. Marion didn't sell as many albums as we thought he would (the Kryger Brothers actually outsold him), which was surprising because Marion came to us with a built-in audience—but I never for a minute regretted having him in our stable. He was a great guy and great musician, and led a great band.

(It's worth noting that Marion was the only artist on our label who played a Chicago brand of polka. The primary quality that differentiates Chicago-style polka from polka on the East Coast is the tempo; those boys from the Midwest played everything considerably more slowly than their East Coast counterparts. Their instrumentation was also slightly different: They liked to use two trumpets, an accordion, a concertina—an accordion-like instrument that looks like a snake when extended to its full length—bass, and drums. The lack of a reed instrument or a keyboard makes their sound far more stripped down, and if I may be honest, while I appreciated what they were doing—and I still do—I enjoy Eastern-style polka better. Even though I recorded and promoted the heck out of Marion, the Chicago polka crowd didn't think much of me. I'll expand on that a little later in the book.)

I also brought Frankie Gutowski into the fold. I used to see Frankie, a native New Jerseyan, perform back at those picnics when I'd skip out on my Little League games, so having him aboard was kind of a thrill. His band was razor-sharp, exciting, and energetic. Frankie wasn't that well-known or popular outside of New Jersey, but if you run your own record label, you have the option to take on passion projects, to record somebody whom you want to record simply because you adore their music. For me, Frankie was that guy.

Every so often I'd stumble into the perfect signing—a great artist with a great band and great following, and a great guy who became a great friend and great musical partner. Starr's most notable perfect signee was none other than Gene Wisniewski.

In the late 1950s and early 1960s, Gene Wisniewski was arguably the most popular performer in all of polka. Gene was a former pilot who fought in World War II. After he got out of the army, Gene formed his band, Gene Wisniewski and His Harmony Bells Orchestra. Within months the Harmony Bells became one of the finest suppliers of Polish-style polka in the country, in part because Gene was a road warrior who toured *constantly*. He brought polka to the people cheerfully, consistently, and energetically. Gene had one of the most loyal fan bases of his era, so it's little wonder that Dana Records, at the height of its popularity, brought him into the studio a number of times. Each of those records was a winner.

I couldn't tell you how, why, or when Gene and I became such close friends. Even though he was considerably older than me (not old enough to be my father, but close enough), we just clicked. Naturally, we spent a lot of time chatting about the polka business, talking shop about the music, the musicians, the road, and the fans; but we also talked about nothing, and I'd rather talk about nothing with Gene than something with a lot of other people.

Even though he never told me, I know for a fact that Gene felt the same way. He had a close friend named Alda Villiard, and Alda once told me, "You know what, Jimmy? Gene told me that he looks at you as the son he never had." And that is a true honor.

Starr Records never released anything by the Harmony Bells Orchestra, but we documented Gene on record as the vocalist for, you guessed it, Jimmy Sturr and His Orchestra. He sang on seven of our records, and I still cite those as my favorites albums from my pre-CD years.

Right when Gene entered into my life, I came up with the brilliant (some might say crazy) idea of recording an album of medleys. And not just medleys composed of two or three songs, but *long* medleys, medleys with some weight to them, medleys that were six, seven, or even ten songs long. It's not as crazy as it might sound: polka fans like to party, and if you have a long string of songs, they'll have the opportunity to dance without a break.

On my first medley record, I pulled together a whopping sixty-six tunes. To give you some perspective, The Beatles, in the band's eight-year career, recorded a total of 304 tunes. I laid down sixty-six in one afternoon. (If I kept up that pace over an eight-year period—we're talking recording three albums every twelve months—you're looking at a total of 1,584 songs, give or take a few.) The album was called *Pure Polka* and it proved why polka experts considered Gene as one of the great singers of his era. Thanks to Gene's tour de force performance, *Pure Polka* helped put me on the map as far as polka was concerned. It got to the point where I had to keep a box of *Pure Polka* in the trunk of my car because it seemed like everywhere I went, somebody would ask, "Hey, ya got a copy of that record with all the songs on it that I can buy from ya?"

I think part of the reason it appealed to everybody was that it was the record with *all the songs*. Hard-core polka fans could enjoy it because it had all their favorites, and newcomers could appreciate it because it was a terrific introduction to the genre. *Pure Polka* was such a hot seller for us that I did a second medleys album, *Make Mine Polkas!* But I upped the ante this time and laid down seventy-seven songs. Nobody who ever bought any of these records complained about not getting their money's worth.

I'm not one to play favorites. If you were to ask me, "Who's your favorite polka band?" my answer would change every six months, depending on who'd just put out a great record or delivered a great live performance. But the fact of the matter is, I like *everybody*. To me, if you're playing the music competently, you're worth listening to.

But that Gene Wisniewski, well, he was something special.

Postscript #1: *No discussion of record labels can be complete without telling the tale of Nino Bruno and Vinnie Dean.*

Vinnie was a jazz saxophonist who recorded and/or toured with the likes of Stan Kenton, Benny Goodman, and Charlie Barnett. Nino, a solid but unspectacular drummer, was one of his closest friends. When Vinnie got off the road with those jazz greats, he convinced Nino to help him launch and run a recording studio in New Rochelle, New York. Nino said yes, and soon after they set up shop, they took off.

Everybody liked working at their place . . . except me. I recorded one album up there and didn't care for it one bit. I couldn't tell you exactly what the problem was—the studio just didn't sound right. (The album was better than that mess I cut for Dyno Records, but anything was better than that.) I didn't have any hard feelings. How could I? You don't know if a studio will work for you unless you give it a shot.

Several years later, my band was playing at a fair in a town called Cobleskill in upstate New York, and who was there in the front row, clapping and dancing like a madman? None other than Nino Bruno himself. After the show, Nino and I filled each other in on our respective recent pasts. He told me that he'd gotten into the horse business (he owned a bunch of quarter horses, and was getting ready to open his own racetrack) and then mentioned, "Vinnie and I are starting to promote records on television. We just did one by this group called the Harmonicats, and it sold fifty-five thousand copies."

That got my wheels spinning. "You know what, Nino? You should think about doing some polka albums. I have something that'll work for you perfectly."

"What's that?"

"I did two albums of medleys. One had sixty-six songs, and the other had seventy-seven. I think you can do something with that."

"Yeah? I think so too. Wait here." And then he ran off. Ten minutes later, he returned and told me, "Vinnie doesn't want to do it . . ."

"Oh," I said. "That's too bad."

". . . but I do."

A couple months later, Nino combined those two albums into one set called Let's Have a Polka Party. When it came out, Vinnie Dean was not pleased . . . that is until the day he called the agency he'd hired to advertise and distribute their records to get the sales figures on the Harmonicats record. After his contact relayed said numbers—numbers that were quite good, mind you—Vinnie asked, "And how's that polka record doing?"

(continued on next page)

(continued from previous page)

The agency guy said, "It's a bomb."

"I knew it. I tried to talk Nino out of doing that. I was sure it would tank. I don't even want to tell you how much money we wasted on that thing."

The agency guy then said, "I'm pulling your leg, Vinnie. The first day it sold about ten thousand copies."

"What?"

"You heard me, ten thousand!"

"What about the second day?" Vinnie asked.

"The second day, it sold a few more thousand, and the day after that, a few thousand more. By the fourth day, it was up to twenty-five thousand! You guys got yourself a hit."

It was Nino and Vinnie's biggest record by far, and it was arguably the most important record of my career. The final tally: 550,000 copies sold. The follow-up, Million Dollar Polkas, sold another 675,000, the third one, Polka Fever, moved a mere 400,000, and the one after that, a holiday record called Polka Christmas in My Hometown, was a comparative stiff at only 300,000. The next one was called Polka Disco, which featured a guest appearance by Donna Summers's drummer. The first four of my records with Nino and Vinnie made them millionaires, but that fifth one, the disco one, well, let's just say that one wasn't quite as successful, and leave it at that.

Postscript #2: While we're on the topic of recording studios . . .

For a good long time, I cut all of my records at RCA Studios in New York, and when the studio closed, I moved over to Clinton Recording Studios. From there I went to a place in Englewood, New Jersey, called Bennett Studios, which was helmed by Tony Bennett's son, Dae. Bennett Studios was a great place to record, partly because Dae was great at his job, and partly because you never knew whom you'd run into.

Back in 2010, while I was cutting one of my polka-fests, the great Tony Bennett himself was in the next recording room over, recording his Duets album with Josh Groban and John Mayer. I ran into Mr. Bennett during one of our respective breaks from recording. We made some small talk over coffee, then, when it was time to get back to work, he said, "You know what, Jimmy? I'm jealous of you."

"You?!" I said. "Jealous of me? You're Tony Bennett, for cryin' out loud. Why would Tony Bennett be jealous of Jimmy Sturr?"

He gave me that brilliant Tony Bennett smile and said, "Because you have eighteen Grammys, and I have only twelve."

Sadly, Bennett Studios was forced to shut its doors in 2011. I'm just glad I got to make some music in that wonderful, wonderful joint.

Postscript #3: No discussion about Starr Records can be complete without mentioning that I was the second artist in polka history to release an eight-track tape. Needless to say, it wasn't one of our biggest moneymakers, but that shouldn't be a surprise because eight-tracks didn't make money for anybody.

But that didn't stop us from pushing the envelope. We were the first polka band to release a gatefold two-album set, a CD, and a DVD, as well as the only polka band to ever release a picture disk. What with today's technology, I don't know how I'll be able to top that. Maybe a Jimmy Sturr and His Orchestra hologram . . .

Jimmy and Myron Floren along with the band, taken in Jimmy's yard with his car.

11

Hey, Niekro!

Now is the moment you've all been waiting for: the Jimmy Sturr history of the knuckleball. (Baseball fans, sit back and enjoy the ride. Non-baseball fans, bear with me because it'll all make sense in a few pages.)

Most modern baseball pitchers have between three or four pitches in their arsenal. Everybody throws a fastball, a curveball, and a changeup, while some folks add in a slider, which is kind of a reverse curveball, or a screwball, which could be called a reverse slider. But at any given time, there are a small handful of guys in Major League Baseball who throw the knuckleball. It's a special pitch, and the guys who call it their specialty are generally special pitchers.

Baseball historians have eternally argued about who threw the first knuckleball. Some say it was the legendary Chicago White Sox hurler Eddie Cicotte, while others believe it was the Philadelphia Phillies' less-than-legendary Lew "Hicks" Moren. Legend has it that when Cicotte threw it he actually held the ball with his thumb and four knuckles, thus the name of the pitch. (Today there aren't any knuckles in a knuckleball—it's gripped with the fingertips.) The point of that was to make certain the ball left Cicotte's hand without any rotation. When the baseball is projected from an arm without any spin, aerodynamics will take over; during its trip between the pitcher's mound and home plate, the air currents, the temperature, and the seams will conspire to make the ball hop, skip, and jump its way to the batter. The pitch is nearly impossible to perfect—that's why so few people throw the darn thing—but if you get it down, you might just have yourself a wonderful career.

In a quirk of fate, two of the greatest knuckleballers in Major League Baseball history were the Niekro brothers, Phil and Joe.

Phil was born in 1939 and made his Major League debut with the old Milwaukee Braves at twenty-five. The young right-hander didn't make much of an impression until 1967, the year after the Braves moved to Atlanta, when he won eleven games against nine losses. In 1967 an 11–9 record wasn't anything to write home about compared to guys like Bob Gibson and Sandy Koufax, who were routinely notching twenty-five victories and fewer than five losses. But Phil stood out due to his league-leading earned run average of 1.87, a number that was astounding even in an era dominated by pitching. For the remainder of his base-ball life, that was pretty much the story: a few more wins than losses and amazing ERAs. Over his twenty-four-year career, Phil managed to win only twenty or more games in a season only three times, but he kept runners off the base paths. His dura-bility was unquestioned, so every team he played for considered themselves lucky to have him on the roster.

Most fans loved Phil Niekro because he threw a knuckleball better than anybody. He was reliable, and even though his career winning percentage was only .537, he was a winner. I loved Phil Niekro because he loved polka.

For me, it all started in 1983 in West Palm Beach, Florida, the spring training home of the Atlanta Braves. I was in town for some gigs; after one of my shows, one of the Braves fans ran over and, breathlessly, said, "Jimmy, you're not gonna believe this, but I found out that Phil Niekro is a fan of yours."

After catching his breath, he added, "Tomorrow afternoon

you're invited to a party. Phil's gonna be there. You guys will get along great." He gave me the address, said, "See you then," and took off.

The next day, after chatting for only a few minutes, Phil and I hit it off famously. Because he was a huge music fan, and I was a huge baseball fan, we had plenty to talk about. Plus, he was just an all-around good guy. We exchanged phone numbers and casually kept in touch, but since we both had jobs that involved a whole lot of traveling, we didn't have the opportunity to see each other until the Braves' off-season, when Phil showed up to my more-or-less-annual Christmas show at Carnegie Hall.

We met up for a bite after the show at Rosie O'Grady's on Seventh Avenue and Fifty-Second Street in Midtown. After finishing up dinner, we walked back to our hotel on the East Side. When we got to Fifth and Forty-Eighth, Phil stopped and said, "Jimmy, I'm going to tell you something that nobody knows about. And you have to promise to keep it quiet."

"My lips are sealed," I said.

"Okay. So I came to New York for two reasons: one, to see your concert, and two, tomorrow morning, I'm signing a contract with the New York Yankees."

I gave him a hug and said, "Welcome to New York, Phil. The Empire State is proud to have you."

Phil was with the Yanks for only two years, but during his brief stint, we grew quite close, so much so that he stayed at my house in Florida during Yankee home stands. (Why, you might ask, would a pitcher of his caliber set up shop that far from Yankee Stadium? Well, at that point, Phil had been in the majors for more than a decade and he didn't feel like he needed to be at the center of everything. He wanted to hang out somewhere quiet, and Florida is nothing if not quiet.) Sometimes he'd drive my car to the stadium, and sometimes I'd tag along, which was always as exciting as heck, no matter how many times I joined him. Pulling up to that stadium and going into the building through the players-only entrance made me feel like I was a little kid again.

Phil and I frequented a bar in Florida called Harter's Hotel, but truth be told, the place wasn't really a hotel; it was more of a shot-and-beer joint with a couple of rooms for rent on the second floor. Harter's was a workingman's place with cheap drinks, thirsty onion farmers, and a jukebox filled with polka music. During his first few appearances there, all the locals harassed Phil, asking him about life as a Major League ballplayer. Eventually the farmers ran out of baseball questions for Phil, so the conversations were dominated with talk about hunting, fishing, and polkas. I'd like to think that the fact that we made Phil feel comfortable and at home was the reason why his two seasons with the Yankees were so successful. (He was 16–8 in 1984 and 16–12 in 1985—not too shabby.)

During the 1984 season, Phil helped arrange to have my band play a few songs at Yankee Stadium on the team's Polish Night. The afternoon of the game, we soundchecked to an empty stadium, which was a treat in and of itself. (Imagine that you're standing on the infield of one of what was then the most vital baseball stadiums in history, playing the music that you love.) But the sense of excitement tripled when, after we wrapped up our first song, I caught a peek of the giant centerfield scoreboard and saw in big, bright letters *"NOW THAT'S MUSIC!!!"*

The next day, we romped through a few tunes as the crowd filed in before the game, a crowd that was totally on our side because those seats were filled with polka fans who were bussed in from the likes of Hartford, Connecticut; Springfield, Massachusetts; and Bethlehem, Pennsylvania. To steal a baseball phrase, we had home-field advantage, and for a few hours, Yankee Stadium became the biggest dance hall in history.

Phil Niekro, number 35, dancing the polka at Yankee Stadium with the band in the background.

The following spring—right in the middle of spring training—our band was playing a show down in West Palm Beach, Florida. During one of our breaks, in came Phil and his brother Joe (the Yankees had signed him during the off-season, much to Phil's pleasure), along with a burly catcher named Ron Hassey, the talented pitcher Dave Righetti, and a utility infielder by the name of Mike Fischlin. The place was mobbed, so I decided that it was the ideal time to goof around with my good friend Phil.

After the first tune of the second set, before the clapping even died down, I picked up the microphone and said, "Thanks for your kind applause, ladies and gentlemen. I have some news for everybody. There are a few members of the New York Yankees with us here tonight, and one of them is the great Phil Niekro. Now everybody knows that Phil throws one hell of a knuckle-ball, but what you might not know is that he's a wonderful clarinet player. Do you want to hear him play a song?" The crowd roared its approval, and I said, "Phil, where are you, buddy? Get on up here and join us for a number or two!" Phil was a good sport, so he made his way up to the front of the room. As he took to the stage, he gave me a funny look, after which I covered the mic and said, "Trust me, it'll be okay. Just go along with me."

While all this was going on, our clarinetist quietly picked up his instrument and a microphone, then walked off stage and ducked behind the curtain. I then handed Phil my clarinet and said, "This song is called 'Clarinet Polka.' You know that one, don't you, pal?" Before Phil could answer, I whispered into his ear, "We've got one of our guys set up backstage with a mic. He's gonna do the song. Just stick the clarinet in your mouth, and then when I count us off, pretend to play." He followed my instructions to a T, and unless someone was paying really, really close attention, it looked like Phil was wailing away on the ol' licorice stick. Since it was a polka party, the drinks were flowing, so I'd venture to say that there weren't too many people paying really, really close attention.

A couple of weeks later, I went to visit Phil at the Yankees spring training location in Fort Lauderdale, Florida, just an hour away from West Palm Beach. I met him outside the stadium, and, after we said our hellos, he said, "You want to come in and see the clubhouse?"

"You bet!" As was the case with most Major League spring training facilities, the clubhouse wasn't nearly as nice as the digs at Yankee Stadium, but I was polite and told Phil how nice it was.

He said, "It's a dump. Want to sit in the dugout?"

"Of course!" A Major League dugout is great, be it spring training or regular season, so while Phil went out for infield practice, I sat down and made myself comfortable. I looked over to my left, and sitting on the other side of the dugout was Whitey Ford, one of the greatest Yankee pitchers of all time. Meeting Eddie Lopat back when I was a kid was incredible, but this, well, this was above and beyond.

That night, Phil, Joe, Righetti, Hassey, Fischlin, and I went out for dinner. After stuffing our faces for a couple of hours, Phil said, "You know what, guys? I just remembered—there's a polka party up in Pompano. Let's go!"

How could I refuse?

The six of us piled into my car and, an hour later, we were sitting at a rickety table in a Knights of Columbus hall in the middle of nowhere, listening to a pretty good little polka band. All of a sudden, I felt a harsh tap on my shoulder. When I turned around, the shoulder-tapper—a tall guy with muscles on top of his muscles—said, "You Jimmy Sturr?"

My first thought was, "Why does this guy want to talk to me when there are all these great ballplayers around?" But I'll talk to anybody, so I said, "I am indeed Jimmy Sturr. And you are?"

He whipped out a badge from his back pocket and said, "I'm from the Fort Lauderdale Police Department. Will you come with me, please?"

Oh. My. God.

When we got to the parking lot, the officer glared at me and said, "Mr. Sturr, it's been reported that you're carrying some illegal drugs in your car."

Now I've been known to have a glass of wine or two, but, to this day, I've never smoked a single joint. Not even a puff. "I think you have the wrong guy, officer," I said.

"I don't. The tip I got was reliable. I have to search your car."

Here's the problem—I didn't own the vehicle I was driving. When I made my winter trip from Florida the town to Florida the state, I borrowed a car from a local elderly friend. I said, "Go ahead, search the car, but please be gentle. It's not mine."

"Yeah, yeah, yeah." After I opened the door, he poked his head in, reached into the glove compartment, and pulled out a baggie filled with white powder. Again glaring at me, he said, "Mr. Sturr, would you care to explain this?"

My chin practically hit the concrete. I became dizzy and could feel the flop sweat dotting my forehead. I knew the bag and its mysterious contents didn't belong to my elderly friend, because, well, he was elderly. I doubted that he was into cocaine, or heroin, or whatever the hell it was. "Officer, that's not mine. Somebody had to have put it there. You have to believe me." I babbled on in that vein for a minute or two, before gathering my wits and saying, "Listen, if you have to book me, please make sure you write on the paperwork that I'm Jim Sturr Jr." My father, of course, was Jim Sturr Sr., and if his name was associated with something like this, he'd kick my ass into tomorrow.

Ignoring me, he said, "Mr. Sturr, you're gonna have to come with me."

The officer took me by the elbow and led me to his police cruiser. At that moment, I noticed the Niekros, Righetti, Hassey, and Fischlin had joined us in front of the club. "Jim," Phil said, "what's going on?"

Putting on a brave face, I said, "There's been some kind of mix-up. This officer here found something in my car that wasn't mine."

Joe asked the cop, "Did you search his car without a warrant? Because if you did, *we* could have *you* arrested."

I knew they'd all had a couple of drinks, so I said, "Joe, don't worry about it. This'll get sorted out."

The cop said, "This is none of your business, boys. Just walk away."

Hassey said, "[Bleep] you, smokey! Get your [bleeping] hands off our friend!"

"Ron," I pleaded, "please stop. This isn't helping . . ."

Phil then piped up, "Quit [bleeping] around with our pal, you [bleep]!"

Fischlin said, "What the [bleep], officer. You can't [bleeping] treat people that [bleeping] way!"

As the cop growled at the players, I could see tomorrow's headline: "YANKEES AND POLKA MUSICIAN ARRESTED AT POLKA PARTY."

"Guys, cool it," I said. "Really, it'll be okay." Or so I hoped.

All five of them ignored me. Instead of cooling it, they heated up and started dropping more F-bombs than I'd ever heard in my life. And then the worst thing that could possibly happen actually happened; Hassey stepped forward and gave the officer a shove.

I didn't want the cop to take a swing at Ron, so as a diversionary measure, I said, "Officer, can you tell me who turned me in?"

He spun on me and said, "No. I'm calling the precinct and letting them know that you and I are on our way into the station." Then he said to my Yankee friends, "Listen, I want all of you guys to shut up and get back inside. You too, Sturr. I'll come and get you when it's time to go. And if you try and pull a runner, you'll just make it worse on yourself. So get in there and wait for me by the bar."

We trudged into the hall, the Yankees continuing the F-bomb barrage the whole way. A minute after we sat down by the bar, the cop burst through the door, got right into my face, and said, "Mr. Sturr, I spoke to my superiors, and you're under arrest . . . unless you buy me a beer."

My Yankee friends then burst out laughing. Turned out that the cop was a huge baseball fan who spent every one of his spare moments watching spring training games and had become friendly with the New York squad. Phil and Joe had planned the whole thing with him days before.

All I could do was say, "You SOBs." Then, because I'm a good sport, and because it never hurts to have friends in high places, I bought the cop a beer.

When the regular season started, Phil decided to forego living in Florida, New York; he moved to New Jersey in order to be close to his brother. They lived in what was then the Loews Glenpointe Hotel, in Teaneck, right off of the Jersey Turnpike. Right about now, you may be asking, "Why would I care where Phil and Joe Niekro lived during the 1985 Major League Baseball season?" Well, I'm about to tell you.

One of the great milestones for a pitcher is winning three hundred games. Since baseball started keeping statistics, only twenty-four men have reached that lofty number. The last guy to do it was Randy Johnson in 2009; as of this writing, no other pitcher is even close. Considering how today's managers rest their hurlers for four games in between starts—up until the beginning of this century, three games was generally the norm—pitchers have fewer opportunities to win games, so there's a possibility it'll never happen again.

Phil won his three-hundredth game on October 6, 1985, against the Toronto Blue Jays. I couldn't be there—and believe me, I wanted to be—because the band was booked for a show in New York City. After the show, when I found out he'd won the game, I told Gussie, who doubled as our bus driver, "Let's go to the Glenpointe."

He said, "But the Yankees are in Toronto. And we have the whole band with us."

I said, "That's fine. It's the last game of the season, and I'm sure they'll do their damnedest to get back to their place ASAP. We'll wait there for them. It won't take too long."

An hour later we pulled into the hotel's parking lot, and I strolled into the lobby. I asked the concierge, who knew me from my numerous previous visits, "Any idea when the Niekros will be back?"

He smiled and said, "They just went upstairs about five minutes ago."

I said, "Great," then I poked my head out of the front entrance and called to the band, "Come on in, boys!"

All twelve of us piled into the elevator and tiptoed down the hall to Phil's room. I knocked on the door, and Joe answered. We shook hands, then I said, "Where's Mr. Three Hundred?"

Cocking his thumb over his shoulder, Joe said, "In the living room, on the phone, talking to the missus."

When he rounded the corner, the entire band burst into a

song I'd written for Phil that appeared on my album *I Remember Warsaw*. The title was, of course, "Hey Niekro!" and the chorus went a little something like this . . .

> *Hey Niekro, hey Niekro*
> *Throw that knuckleball*
> *Strike 'em out, we'll all go home*
> *But we'll stop at the Polish hall*
> *And if he thinks he can keep up*
> *And if he wants to go*
> *Tomorrow night when we return*
> *We'll bring your brother Joe*

Phil burst into tears, hugged each and every one of us, then said, "Gentlemen, let's go downstairs. Drinks are on me!"

And the drinks *were* on him. Many, many drinks, the majority of which were a concoction called moon shooters, whose ingredients are forgotten by everyone who was there, probably because we all drank too many of them. After the hotel bar closed at ten, Phil said, "Come on, guys. The celebration has to continue because I'm pretty sure I don't have another three hundred wins in me. I know another place down the street that'll still be open. It's called the E Street Bar. Let's go!"

We all hopped onto our bus and drove the few blocks to the E Street. Since it was well after midnight on a work night, the bar was relatively empty, but when the owner saw that we had the Niekro boys in tow, he got on the phone and called everybody in his Rolodex. Before we knew it, the place was jam-packed; looking around at all the smiling faces, I pulled Gussie aside and said, "I have an idea."

He took the bus keys from his pocket and said, "You want to get our instruments and play for the people, don't you?"

"Indeed I do!"

We played our first note at 10:25 and didn't pack up until three in the morning. Phil later told me that our performance made it the perfect night.

And you know what? I couldn't have agreed with him more.

Postscript: *Phil's love for polka spread to his entire family; Joe was a huge fan, and his parents were so enamored with the music that Phil arranged for my band to play at the celebration for their fiftieth wedding anniversary in their backyard in Lansing, Ohio. (At the party, I learned that that tiny street in Lansing was one of the most important streets in sports history, as Phil and Joe weren't the only great professional athletes to call it home. Boston Celtics legend John Havlicek grew up across the way, and Pittsburgh Pirates mainstay Bill Mazeroski lived just down the block. It was like the Polish Sports Hall of Fame.)*

Phil was so pleased with the way things went that night that when he was elected to the Hall of Fame in 1997, he invited my band to perform. Unfortunately, I was booked for another job and I couldn't get the bigwigs at the National Baseball Hall of Fame to change the date of the induction ceremony.

12

Polish Hall Madness

Being an entrepreneurial spirit—and being the kind of guy who gets antsy if I have too much free time on my hands—I took almost every musical job that came my way: outdoor festivals, fairs, weddings, bar mitzvahs, and anything else. If somebody wanted polka, I'd happily supply it. The type of affair meant nothing to me because as far as I was concerned, if people wanted to hear polka music, who was I to refuse them? That said, one of my favorite things to do was to create jobs that hadn't previously existed, to have people hire me when they didn't even know they wanted or needed a band.

For instance, a friend of mine, Gussie Zygmunt, owned a bar just outside of Florida called the Crystal Inn. The Crystal was busy almost every day of the year, except the evenings you wouldn't expect a bar to be busy, like late on Christmas night, or the evening of New Year's Day, or Easter Sunday night. It dawned on me that somewhere out in Florida and points beyond, there might be some people looking to cap off their holiday celebration with some polka, so one Thanksgiving night, I asked Gussie if he'd be interested in having a scaled-down version of my band—a trio rather than the full octet—play for a few hours.

Once word got out around town, polka fans were waiting outside for hours until they could squeeze into the restaurant. We'd start playing at 10 p.m. and go until 2 a.m. or beyond, just me, an accordion player, and a drummer. We'd blow through medley after medley, taking on such polka classics as "Ballroom Polka," "Jasui," "Oh Dana," "Apples, Peaches, Pumpkin Pie," "Clarinet Polka," "Violins Play for Me," "Caroline Polka," "Tic-Tock Polka," "Siwy Kon," "Saxo Polka," "Pennsylvania Polka," "My-T-Peppy Polka," "Our Mary," "Tam Pod Krakowem," "Our Gang," "Hosa Horasa," "Wish I Were Single Again," "Red Lantern," "Hu-La-La Polka," "Apples Polka," "Rising Sun Polka," "Domino Polka," "Zlonczki Na Lacze," "Happy Birthday Polka," "Fire Polka," and "Na Zdrowie/Lovers Polka." The crowds drank and danced and drank and sang along and drank some more. A ripping good time was had by all.

And those were some big-money gigs! I paid my sidemen twenty dollars each, and since I was the leader, I gave myself twenty-five dollars.

But bar jobs were far from the norm. Before I started winning Grammy Awards, the majority of my gigs were dances, and the majority of the dances were wedding receptions that were held at dance halls, or as they were referred to around our area, Polish halls. These Polish halls were generally big, empty spaces that held about three hundred people. Most of them weren't particularly fancy or ornate—they didn't have chandeliers or bay windows or gold leaf on the ceiling, but rather they were simple, no-frills places where you could host a raucous party.

As Jimmy Sturr and His Orchestra grew in popularity, we played fewer and fewer Polish hall gigs, which was bittersweet. On one hand, it was wonderful to take the next step up the ladder of the music world, to perform for three, or four, or ten, or a hundred times as many listeners. On the other hand, there was something special about the intimacy of helping a bridal party celebrate its magical day.

(A brief digression for you audiophiles out there. Very, very few of those Polish clubs came equipped with a sound system, so we had to haul our own P.A. from show to show. That was an arduous task, but as least we knew that the shows would be well mixed. Today, even though the majority of our performances are at venues that feature their own sound systems, we still always take that unwieldy P.A. system with us, just in case the one waiting for us isn't satisfactory. I'll always take that route because I *never* want anybody to come up to me after a show and say, "You guys sure looked good up there, but I couldn't hear a thing.")

There were things that happened at Polish clubs that could never happen at, say, the Grand Ole Opry. One night, while this then twenty-one-year-old was still living at home with my parents, I was playing a show at an armory not too far from the house. It was a special evening for me because one of my close friends from New Jersey—a friend whom I didn't see nearly enough—had make the drive up. I put a little something extra into my performance that night because I wanted to make sure he felt the trip had been worthwhile.

After the show, a beautiful young woman sidled up to me, put her hand on my arm, and, in a breathy voice, told me, "I really loved your band. *Really* loved it."

We spoke for about ten minutes, then, being young and brazen, I gave her my parents' address and phone number—my parents were out of town that week—and said, "Come on over in a couple of hours. The back door is unlocked. Come in, go up the stairs, and my bedroom is the first door to the left."

Her eyes lit up. She said, "Okay. I'll see you soon." Then she gave me a kiss on the cheek and skipped off.

A minute later, my Jersey friend wandered over and said, "She was cute. Listen, I'm starved. Let's go grab some grub."

"Sounds good to me," I said, and off we went to a nearby diner. After a two-plus-hour meal filled with bad jokes, great laughter, and a couple of drinks, I looked at my watch and said, "You know what? It's after midnight. It'd be ridiculous for you to drive all the way back up to Jersey. My parents are out of town, and I have the place to myself. How about you come on back to the house and stay the night. You can have my room. I'll take my parents' bed."

"Jimmy," my pal slurred, "you're a prince among men."

By the time we got home, it was well after 2 a.m. I set up my friend in my bedroom, then, exhausted and possibly a tad inebriated, I staggered into my parents' bed. I was asleep before my head hit the pillow. About two hours later, the phone rang. *Who the hell's calling at this hour?*, I wondered, then picked up the handset and grumbled, "H'lo."

"Where were you?!" It was a female voice, and that voice wasn't the least bit happy.

I rubbed my eyes and asked, "Whozis?"

"I'm the girl you met at the dance, dummy. Where were you? I went to your house, just like you said, and I went up to your room, just like you said, and I got undressed, and got into your bed, and it wasn't you!"

I sat up as if I'd been stabbed in the backside with a knitting needle. "What happened when you got into the bed?"

"Nothing! He didn't even wake up!" She hung up on me, hard. Unsurprisingly, I never heard from her again.

And then there was a dance we played in Brooklyn, New York.

It was Halloween night, and our drummer was sick as could be, but, as would be the case with pretty much anyone in the band, he sucked it up and made the gig. Not only did he show up ready to play but he had enough energy to put on a Halloween costume. (For some reason, he decided to dress as a colonial aristocrat, complete with a three-pointed hat and knickers. I still have no idea why.)

When he got onto the bus, the rest of the guys gave him a long, sarcastic round of applause. Coughing, he said, "Thank you, thank you, thank you. So listen, guys, I have this killer cold and just got these new covers for my drums, so be careful."

When we got to the club, our revolutionary war hero set up his drum set, and, with the help from a couple of band members, neatly piled his cases behind his kit. Much to his credit—and much to my pleasure and relief—he rose to the occasion and played wonderfully.

During the show, in between songs, one of my instrumentalists, who shall remain nameless, tapped me on the shoulder and said, "Jimmy, give me a few minutes before the next song. I've gotta take a leak."

I said, "Why didn't you go before we went on stage?" (Sometimes being a bandleader is like being a kindergarten teacher.)

One look into his bloodshot, watery eyes and it was quite apparent that he'd downed a drink or five. Great. "I dunno," he mumbled. "I just didn't. It'll take, like, one minute."

"We have to keep playing. Take your seat," I said, then I counted off the next tune.

He glared at me, then stomped behind the band, unzipped his fly, and began to urinate . . . all over the drummer's new cases. When we left, the drummer left the covers on the stage. I can't say I blamed him, because who wants to walk around with urine-soaked drum covers?

We had some great times at those Polish halls and tiny clubs of the Northeast; while some of those shows could be frustrating, I wouldn't trade the experiences for anything. But after the Grammys started coming in, that sort of monkey business mostly went right out the window.

13

The Grammys

Over the last two decades, the Grammy Awards have gotten a bad rap. For a good twenty-five or thirty years after they originated in 1958, the Grammy was a sought-after prize, a special, one-of-a-kind honor that rewarded an artist for his or her unbeatable combination of excellence and popularity. In the beginning, the voters bestowed Album of the Year honors to the *legitimate* Album of the Year, regardless of the genre. Here's a list of the first seven winners: Henry Mancini, Frank Sinatra, Bob Newhart, Judy Garland, Vaughn Meader, Barbara Streisand, and João Gilberto and Stan Getz. We're talking a composer, a crooner, two comedians, two chanteuses, and a guitarist and jazz saxophonist. Diversity, originality, and quality, with little regard for trendiness. Even though the last seven Albums of the Year have been nearly as diverse—stadium rockers U2, country crooners the Dixie Chicks, jazzer Herbie Hancock, the killer combination of Robert Plant and Alison Krauss, pop/country singer Taylor Swift, alternative rockers Arcade Fire, and retro soul shouter Adele—the Grammys have lost much of their luster. People in and out of the music industry have their theories as to the cause, but I believe folks are less respectful of the Grammys because it's now perceived as a politics-drenched popularity contest, in which the voters are more concerned about casting their ballot for either a million-record seller or for a close, personal friend.

Whether or not any of that is true is debatable, but as they say, perception is reality.

Because I was a professional musician, I had to pay at least a little bit of attention to the Grammy Awards—it's part of the job to know who's capturing the industry's fancy, regardless of genre—but I never went out of my way to watch the ceremonies on television; if I missed the show, I'd just read the results in the newspaper. But in 1985 when the National Academy of Recording Arts and Sciences (NARAS), the Grammy Awards' governing body, added a category for Best Polka Album into the mix, I started paying a lot of attention. I didn't necessarily think I had a chance to even be nominated, let alone win (I was, after all, as I told Cousin Brucie, just a country bumpkin), but there was always the chance it could happen.

Much to my surprise, it *did* happen. Actually, surprise is an understatement. Shock is probably more accurate.

When I was leading the first edition of the Jimmy Sturr Orchestra, the thought of winning any kind of major music award never even entered my mind. I was playing polka music for the sheer joy of performing, and besides, the baseball trophies on the mantel were all the accolades I needed. Even when I was recording album after album after album, and playing my 204 shows a year, I never imagined that anybody in the music industry would give us a second thought. But they did, and when the notices from outside the polka world started trickling in, I embraced it. I suspect that any musician, no matter how jaded he or she may be about the Grammy Awards or the voting process, would feel the same way. When I hear an artist say, "I don't care about the awards one iota. It's all about the work," I think he's lying through his teeth. If you're not at least a little bit honored by a nomination, you're missing something inside.

My first nomination was in 1986 for my record *I Remember Warsaw*. I was up against two great musicians and their great albums: Frankie Yankovic's *America's Favorites* and *Another Polka Celebration* by Eddie Blazonczyk's Versatones. Frankie, who passed away the following year, was one of the best-known polka musicians in the country, partly because he'd been playing great music for decades, and partly due to the popularity of his nonrelative "Weird Al" Yankovic. (By the way, Al chose the name "Yankovic" as his stage name because his parents were huge fans of Frankie's.) *America's Favorites* is loaded with several classics that my band has been playing for decades — "Pennsylvania Polka" and "Too Fat Polka" are two that come to mind — and it was a terrific album, more than worthy of the acclaim.

(A brief digression about Frankie Yankovic. Despite the title of this book, Frankie was, is, and always will be the first "Polka King." Before he passed away in 1998, he played a Slovenian style of polka, which is a bit slower tempo and accordion-heavy. In the late 1940s, Frankie had a couple of massive hits with "Just Because" and "Blue Skirt Waltz." Then in his heyday, he recorded for Columbia Records, and his face was in every record store in the country, right next to fellow Columbia labelmates like Tony Bennett and Miles Davis. Even though Frankie wasn't a direct influence on my music, I have the utmost respect for his work ethic and was proud to have him sit in with the band at several shows. I was even prouder to call him a friend.)

It's not every day that a country bumpkin like me is welcomed into the music industry's inner circle, so I flew to Los Angeles two days before the show in order to soak up as much atmosphere as possible. The night before the ceremony, I was invited to a cocktail party where virtually all of the guests were nominees and I met *everybody* — Paul Simon, Bruce Hornsby, Andre Previn, Jim Henson, Ronnie Milsap, Doc Watson, and Doc Severinsen (who lived just outside of Florida), to name a few. I don't think too many of these folks knew who the heck I was (for that matter, I wouldn't be surprised if some of them knew anything about my genre beyond "Beer Barrel Polka"), but they were all gracious and kind, and made me feel like I belonged.

Up until the morning of the show, I wasn't too concerned about whether or not I'd take home the award, but from the moment I woke up until the moment the award was announced at the chilly Shrine Auditorium, one thought kept running through my head: *Am I gonna win? Am I gonna win? Am I gonna win?* I didn't have my heart set on winning, but if I did, well, I sure wouldn't complain. It turned out Eddie and I garnered an equal number of votes, so we both took home a trophy, and I loved that. As far as I was concerned, *every* polka nominee should get a Grammy.

As I walked up the aisle toward the stage (shivering the whole way because it had to be sixty degrees in there), it dawned on me that virtually all of the other award winners had thanked God for helping get them to this point. So after I went through my list of acknowledgments, I wrapped it up by saying, "Finally, like everybody else here tonight, I'd like to thank the Lord for helping me win this award . . . but I'd also like to ask him if he could turn down the air conditioner." It brought down the house.

The following year, 1987, I got the nod for *Please Have Them Play a Polka Just for Me,* one of my first recordings with The Jordanaires. (That's The Jordanaires, as in Elvis Presley's background vocalists. More about them later.) That was an especially enjoyable outing because it featured some newer tunes, recent additions to the book such as "Cajun Creole," "Cedar Stump," and "Scolding Mother." Eddie got another nomination for *Let's Celebrate Again.* Our competition was Lenny Gomulka and Dick Pillar for their sharp album *In Polka Unity,* Walt Groller's terrific *Polkamatic,* and *Polka Mania* from former Starr Records artists the

Jimmy accepting one of his Grammy Awards.

Kryger Brothers. This time I managed to get a few more votes than Eddie and took home a Grammy that I didn't have to share.

In 1988 my set *Born to Polka* was nominated, a record that, like *Please Have Them Play* . . . , featured some newer songs like "Sweet Rosie Kowalski," "Polish and So Proud," and "The Devil's Fiddle." Lenny Gomulka and his own band, Chicago Push, were honored for *Join the Polka Generation*, an album that it saddens me to say is currently out of print. (I have my own copy, thank you very much. If you promise to return it to me in perfect condition, I might even lend it to you.) Joining us were Jimmy Weber and the Sounds with *Sounds from a Polka Party*, Stas Bulanda's Average Polka Band with *Let's Have a Party*—apparently 1988 was a good year for parties—and Walter Ostanek and his Band's *All Aboard, It's Polka Time*. Known as Canada's "Polka King," Walter is one of the best, and topping him for the award was kind of bittersweet. (If I'm being honest, though, it was a little more sweet than bitter!)

Walter and I were up against each other again the following year; I had *All in My Love for You*, and he had *Any Time Is Polka Time*. Our competition was Gene Mendalski and the G-Men and the raucous *Moldie Oldie Golden Goodies,* Gordon Hartmann and his cleverly named *Polkaholic*, and *Penn Ohio Polka Pals Souvenir Edition* by, you guessed it, the Penn Ohio Polka Pals. Those were four excellent, excellent recordings, and I was frankly surprised that I pulled that one out, but I was also ecstatic to have my third Grammy.

The year 1992 saw a showdown between me and my friendly rivals, Eddie Blazonczyk with *All Around the World*, and Jimmy Weber with *Sounds from the Heart*. The other two groups were the Polka Family Band and Toledo Polkamotion, a band that sounded good both in and out of Ohio. Before the show, I figured that at this point, the Grammy voters might be sick of me, so I fully expected Eddie to snatch up the award. But, surprisingly, I did it again! I suspect that it had something to do with the fact that the album, *Live at Gilley's!*, was, as you might guess from the title, recorded in concert. It's not every day you come across a live polka album from Gilley's.

In 1992 for the first time, I didn't win the Grammy for which I was nominated, even though the album, *Sturr It Up*, featured "The Greatest Day in Baseball," a song I really liked. (Not that I don't like all my songs, mind you, but anytime I can do something that involves baseball is extra special.) Walter Ostanek took that year's award . . . and the next . . . and the next. Everybody says it's an honor just to be nominated—and it was, it was!—but when *I Love to Polka* earned me the 1995 Grammy, well, I have to admit that it felt pretty good to win again.

The Grammy nominations were announced during the winter months, which meant that I was generally down south in the state of Florida. After 1995 for nomination day, I got into the habit of getting a bunch of friends together and hitting a restaurant in Jupiter called Jetty's for the big announcement. We'd eat and drink, and I'd stare at my cell phone, waiting for Gussie to call and say either "Congratulations!" or "You didn't make it." No matter how often I got "Congratulations!" it never got old; for that matter, it actually got more exciting every year.

I won the next three in a row—'96, '97, and '98—for, respectively, *Polka! All Night Long*, *Living on Polka Time*, and *Dance with Me*, and while it's impossible to pick my favorite Grammy—it's like picking your favorite child—these were among the top five. They were such fun albums to make because they featured guest appearances by some of my favorite musicians of all time—Willie Nelson and Bill Anderson to name two—but also because the competition was at such a high level. Eddie, Lenny, Walter, and Frankie were among the usual suspects, and they were at the top of their games, believe me. I honestly thought the 1999 award deservedly went to Brave Combo, a hip group from Texas that brought a harder rock feel to the polka party.

Between 2000 and 2008 the award for Best Polka Album was taken home by either Brave Combo or yours truly, with Combo winning in 2000 and 2004. (I wasn't actually nominated in 2005, which I found odd, because I felt like my 2004 album, *Rock 'n' Polka*—which featured the likes of Lee Greenwood, Duane Eddy, Willie Nelson, and Alison Krauss helping me cover such rock, pop, and soul classics as "Splish Splash," "Personality," "Fun, Fun, Fun," "Don't Be Cruel," and "Since I Met You Baby"— was my best one of the 2000s. But you can't get nominated every year, I guess.) Chronologically, my albums that were honored were called *Polka! All Night Long, Touched by a Polka, Gone Polka, Top of the World, Let's Polka 'Round, Shake, Rattle and Polka!, Polka in Paradise, Come Share the Wine,* and *Let the Whole World Sing,* and each had a special place in my heart.

Fans and reporters all over the world have asked me if the process ever got boring or repetitive, and my answer is always a resounding, emphatic *no.* It took a long time and a lot of hard work, long bus rides to shows performed at tiny venues for only a handful of people, and more self-promotion than I care to discuss. But when you have tangible proof that the music industry is paying attention not just to you but to the music you've lived and breathed for your entire career, well, that could never get boring.

For reasons that were never made clear to me, NARAS eliminated the Best Polka Album award after the 2008 ceremonies. Right now, after a couple years of being shifted from one genre to another, we're lumped into the category for Best Regional Roots Music. In 2011 my record *Not Just Another Polka* was nominated, but instead of sharing the honor with the likes of Lenny, Walter, and Brave Combo, I was up against two Zydeco greats, C.J. Chenier and Steve Riley, a Hawaiian guitar virtuoso named George Kahumoku Jr., and the eventual winner, New Orleans's wonderful Rebirth Brass Band. When I heard the nominees, I knew that would be the end. There's no way that a polka artist—*any* polka artist—could compete against a hugely popular, hugely visible group like Rebirth, or an accessible, popular artist like C.J. I'm still disappointed that polka probably won't have its own Grammy category ever again, but when I'm feeling down about it, all I need to do is look at those eighteen awards displayed behind the bar in my living room, and think about how lucky I am.

Postscript #1: *After that first Grammy Award, calls started pouring in from major booking agents who'd likely never thought about hiring a polka band in their lives, and while I don't have official statistics, I'd estimate that over the twelve months after I won my first Grammy, I played twice as many shows as the year before. We played fairs all across the country, fairs that, until I brought home that statue, had probably never heard of me.*

For example, there was an agency in Ohio called Variety Attractions that started landing me jobs as far west as North and South Dakota. I mean, while I was playing all those shows up and down

(continued on next page)

(continued from previous page)

the East Coast, I never dreamed that the band would get beyond Illinois, let along the Midwest and beyond.

The venues got bigger, the crowds got louder, and the shows, if I can brag a little bit, got even better. Those Grammy trophies sure look shiny and pretty up on the shelves above the little bar in my living room, but as beautiful as they are, the most important thing about winning those awards is that it gave my career a boost that I'll be feeling until the day I hang up my clarinet and sax.

Postscript #2: I might get in trouble for saying this, but what the heck . . .

I believe part of the reason that NARAS dissolved the Best Polka Album category was because it didn't want a polka artist to be the biggest Grammy winner of all time. (As of this writing, I'm number six on the list.) Before polka was melded with the Regional Roots Album category in 2011, we spent a couple years with the folk albums, and NARAS's reasoning for that was thin at best: It claimed that there weren't enough polka entries to merit a category. Now if you go into my basement, look at my record collection, and see how many polka albums were released in 2008, 2009, or whatever year it was that this backroom decision was made, you'd realize that that's plain ridiculous.

Much to my surprise, and probably much to somebody's chagrin, I earned a Best Contemporary Folk nomination in 2009. Even though I didn't win, I feel that somebody in the NARAS braintrust thought, "We can't have this Sturr fella getting another award. Let's lump him in with Roots. He'll have no chance to get nominated there."

Shows what they knew.

In 2010 they stuck me in with the pop artists, which was so absurd, I had to say something. I gave NARAS a call and, after being *passed around to about four different secretaries, I finally found the right person. "Why am I in with the Lady Gagas of the world?" I asked.*

"Well, Mr. Sturr, um, you see, the committee feels that your music is too smooth to fit in with the folkies."

"Too smooth?" I asked.

"Yes. Too smooth."

There's no such thing as smooth polka. Polka is raucous and jagged and exciting and fun. That was just a convenient excuse. I know they were lying because I had friends who were members of NARAS, and they were given the opportunity to cast their ballots for other polka records in the Contemporary Folk category.

I've said it before and I'll probably say it again: I may be a country bumpkin, but don't ever try to pull the wool over my eyes. If you don't want me to win another Grammy, just tell me. I'll be a bit sad, but it won't stop me from making records and trying to make those records into the best records they can be.

14

Causing More Trouble

I might have ruffled a few feathers with that little Grammy rant in the previous chapter, and if you were offended or upset about anything I said, I apologize, especially if you're a NARAS voter who has nothing to do with the big decisions that affect how the awards are given out. But now I'm going to make some waves in my neck of the woods.

In the interest of accuracy, here's what the International Polka Association (IPA) has to say about itself. And the text below comes directly from its website (www.internationalpolka.com) so the association won't be able to complain about being misquoted or misrepresented:

> *The concept of a national polka convention had been developed and pioneered originally in Chicago. From the popular yearly moonlight dances starting in 1960, which attracted thousands of polka lovers from all sections of the United States and Canada – the first polka convention emerged in 1963. This developed into the International Polka Convention which was presented each succeeding year in Chicago, Detroit and Buffalo, New York.*
>
> *In January, 1968 a steering committee comprised of Johnny Hyzny, Leon Kozicki, Joe and Jean Salomon, Eddie Blazonczyk and Don Jodlowski met to discuss plans for the next convention. After a series of meetings they began preparations for the*

formation of the International Polka Association. The Association was officially chartered by the State of Illinois as a "not for profit" corporation and was registered with the County of Cook (Chicago) in August of 1968.

Since 1968 the International Polka Festival has been presented under the auspices of the International Polka Association. The delegates to the 1968 Convention approved the establishment of the Polka Music Hall of Fame and the presentation of annual Polka Music Awards.

As stated in its charter, the International Polka Association was organized as: "An educational and charitable organization for the preservation, promulgation and advancement of polka music and; to promote, maintain and advance public interest in polka entertainment; to advance the mutual interests and encourage greater cooperation among its members who are engaged in polka entertainment; and to encourage and pursue the study of polka music, dancing and traditional folklore."

The International Polka Association presents many special awards each year to encourage the promotion of polka music. Through the efforts of the IPA, the month of January has been proclaimed as National Polka Music Month and the annual festival has served as a show place for new, deserving polka talent. Many functions under the auspices of the IPA are presented in various states, a weekly radio program has been established and a monthly news bulletin keeps the members informed of the business affairs of the Association, as well as polka related events and news from across the country.

The International Polka Association is also responsible for the continued operation and growth of the Polka Music Hall of Fame and Museum. It is through this branch that the Association has been able to continue its historical, educational and research goals on behalf of the polka music industry.

In spite of the fact that I've spent most of my adult life trying to raise polka awareness, to the International Polka Association, I'm a black sheep. Unlike my old radio nemesis, the Irish-fearing Ron Kurowski, the IPA doesn't care that I'm not Polish. In this case, the association's issue with me is my style of music. According to the IPA, its style is the only style. As noted, Midwestern polka and Northeastern polka are radically different schools of thought, but that shouldn't mean they can't coexist, right? Not according to the IPA.

The association also takes issue with my choice to mine other genres for interesting songs and incorporate these non-polka tunes into our repertoire. Now, I'm all for traditionalism, but not everybody likes traditional polka, and this kind of attitude might exclude people who can't decide whether or not they want to take the polka plunge. The International Polka Association is entitled to its opinion, of course, but what sense does it make for a musical subculture like ours to snipe at one another? Wouldn't it be more productive if we all pulled in the same direction? Snobbishness or personal preference shouldn't be a factor in how you run your organization, especially if your organization is one that's supposed to support the arts. Our only concern should be banding together and figuring out how to build and nurture the largest fan base we can.

To that end, back in the day, I was a big supporter and promoter of the IPA. From the very beginning of my career, even when I was a kid, I'd talk up the organization at appropriate shows, try to recruit members, and just generally spread the good word. In exchange for all of my good work, I'd receive a halfhearted invitation to perform at its annual convention. Actually, it wasn't even an invitation—it was a request to submit a bid to perform, meaning IPA wanted to find out how much I'd charge for my services, and if I fit into the budget, maybe, just maybe IPA would consider thinking about deciding whether or not I should possibly be asked to play. Even after filling out the form year after year, I never received a call back.

At first, I assumed IPA wasn't responding because my bids were too high, so I asked a bandleader friend of mine who'd played at several of the IPA conventions if he'd feel comfortable telling me the amount of his paycheck. He gladly did, so the next year, I put in a bid below his bid that had been accepted the previous year. Nothing. The next year, I lowered the bid again. Still nothing. The next year, I cut it all the way down to $1,200, which wouldn't even cover transporting my band from New York to Chicago and back again. Somebody actually phoned me that time . . . to tell me that IPA couldn't afford it. Being a never-say-die sort, the next year, I told the association that all it would need to do is cover my band's hotel rooms.

Again, the answer was no. I may not be the sharpest tool in the onion patch, but if you tell me something over and over again, eventually I'll get the point.

I don't know how or why it happened, but in 1984, I was voted into the IPA Hall of Fame. Again, in the interest of accuracy, here's what the IPA website has to say about the Hall of Fame:

> For too long of a time those of us who enjoy polka music had neglected to bestow proper honor and recognition to performers, deejays, and others who have rendered years of faithful service to the polka entertainment industry. Through the years there was considerable discussion and research among our polka leaders to formulate an institution that would honor deserving polka personalities. Although there always was complete agreement as to the purpose and objectives of such an institution, there also existed the reluctance of any group to accept the challenge and responsibility.

To rectify this omission of duty, the delegates to the 1968 International Polka Convention voted and approved the establishment of the Polka Music Hall of Fame. The institution of the Hall of Fame serves to honor outstanding polka personalities who have made significant contributions to the advancement and promotion of polka music. After many months of research and development, the much talked about and long overdue Polka Music Hall of Fame became a living reality. The following year Frankie Yankovic and Li'l Wally Jagiello became the first Hall of Famers elected. They were honored in Chicago at a banquet and special installation ceremony.

The Polka Music Hall of Fame is administered by an eleven member Board of Trustees. Since originally being established it has undergone several changes. Recipients of this coveted honor are determined by the votes of an academy of over 165 qualified electors. Each year they elect two prominent living polka personalities and one deceased polka personality, who have made outstanding contributions to the advancement and promotion of polka music. Another personality is elected in the pioneer category. Candidates must have been actively engaged in the polka field for a minimum of twenty years. They are selected from all sections of the United States and Canada regardless of ethnic origin, locality or style preference of polka music. The nationally known Institute of Industrial Relations of Loyola University of Chicago has been retained yearly to conduct the election and certify the winners. In conjunction with the Polka Music Hall of Fame, the IPA also presents the annual Polka Music Awards for the favorite performers of the year.

In compliance with the commitment to establish the Polka Music Hall of Fame, the International Polka Association has provided continuous financial support for the improvement *and expansion of the Polka Music Hall of Fame and Museum —a dream that became a reality. A suitable and functional building to serve as the depository for the Polka Music Hall of Fame, Museum and administrative office of the Association was purchased.*

Later, due to changing circumstances, the building housing the Hall of Fame and Museum was sold and the associated memorabilia is now housed at 4608 S. Archer Avenue, Chicago, in property owned by Polonia Banquets, where board and general membership meetings are also held.

In addition to its function of honoring deserving personalities, the Polka Music Hall of Fame and Museum also serves as a historical and educational medium for polka music. The Hall of Fame and Museum provide a means for people to learn about the origins and development of polka music in all its styles and forms. It also provides an historical record of events and occurrences in the polka field. The institution also contains an unparalleled collection of artifacts, sheet music, recordings and memorabilia associated with polka music that not only provides an educational resource for the general public, but is also a research tool for scholars, the media and historians.

That all sounds good, doesn't it? Sounds like IPA really has a lot of love and respect for its inductees, right? So if IPA were offering honorary lifetime memberships to certain current Hall of Fame members—one of whom had managed to win a Grammy Award or two—it would jump at the chance to hitch its wagon to his star. Well, in the early 2000s, the names of ten polka greats were submitted to an IPA special committee as deserving of this lifetime membership, one of whom was yours truly.

I heard through a reliable source that one of the committee members looked at the list, then said, "Jimmy Sturr? What did he ever do for us? Everybody's in except for him. All in favor?" The vote against me was unanimous.

And that, my friends, is the true meaning of "Chicago style."

15

Rounder and Rounder

The majority of my albums that were honored with Grammys were waxed and distributed by one of the great record labels of its time, Rounder Records. It was an ideal place for a guy like me to be, because Rounder knows its music and has a superb collection of people. The folks there are professional, they're kind, and they have a rebel spirit about them; they don't care what genre you perform in, what you look like, or how many records you'd previously sold. If Rounder likes your music, it'll sign you and promote you to the best of its abilities.

The sheer number and stylistic range of artists Rounder has had on its roster since it was founded in 1970 is staggering: blues cats such as Marcia Ball, Solomon Burke, Jimmie Dale Gilmore, Clarence "Gatemouth" Brown, James Booker, and Ronnie Earl; alternative and rock acts like Robert Plant, John Mellencamp, NRBQ, The Tragically Hip, Lisa Loeb, They Might Be Giants, J. Geils Band, Dennis DeYoung, and Juliana Hatfield; such Cajun greats as Buckwheat Zydeco; country artists including Cowboy Junkies and Roy Book Binder; jazz folks like the Dirty Dozen Brass Band, David Grisman, and Béla Fleck; and even the periodic classical composer like Philip Glass. That sense of diversity is undoubtedly why it decided to take a chance on a polka guy from a tiny town in New York. The fact that I'd developed a following of my own over the years didn't hurt.

Rounder was founded in 1970 by a trio of like-minded music nuts named Ken Irwin, Bill Nowlin, and Marian Leighton-Levy. (It should be noted that when they launched the label, all three were still in college. Being a former young entrepreneur, those are some people I can get behind.) They named the label Rounder in homage to one of their favorite folk bands, a Greenwich Village cult group called the Holy Modal Rounders. See? Music nuts.

In the beginning, Rounder was better known as a distributor than a label, and if anybody can respect and understand how difficult it is to balance the two, it's yours truly, but Rounder managed to do it, arguably better than anybody else in its era. In addition to producing early-career records from the likes of Allison Krauss and George Thorogood and the Destroyers, it managed to distribute more than four hundred labels. I just had to distribute one label, and that in and of itself was a huge headache.

I consider my series of records for Rounder to be among the most creatively fulfilling of my career. For the most part, *Polka Your Troubles Away, I Love to Polka, Living on Polka Time, Polka! All Night Long, Dance with Me, Polkapalooza, Touched by a Polka, Gone Polka, Top of the World, Let's Polka 'Round, Rock 'n' Polka, Shake, Rattle and Polka!, Polka in Paradise, Come Share the Wine,* and *Let the Whole World Sing* were radically different than my Starr Records sessions. The recording budgets were higher, the guest artists were more well-known, and the song selection was far more diverse. While the label brass gave me periodic creative suggestions, I never felt pressured to do what they said. They gave me as much artistic freedom as I could hope for (I'm sure that every Rounder artist you'd speak to would say the same thing), and this is why I'll always have fond memories of my fifteen years with the label. It's nice to have the autonomy of bringing my own records to fruition, but if I ever decide that running my own music empire gets to be a bit much, and that it would be easier to let some professionals handle the heavy lifting, I'll reach out to my friends at Rounder.

In what I'm certain was an easy decision, Rounder got out of the distribution business (wearing both hats dilutes both ends of the business; focusing on one aspect is both easier and more fruitful); in 2010, Rounder sold to the Concord Music Group in California. While the main thrust of Concord's business is jazz, the company champions the kind of diversity that Rounder is known and loved for, and I think it's a perfect marriage. I haven't been a part of the Rounder family for several years now (it was an amicable split), but I have nothing but good things to say about Ken and his crew.

16

Country and Polka: The Perfect Marriage

If you listened to a Hank Williams record right after hearing a Myron Floren record, you wouldn't necessarily think, *Hmm, Myron was influenced by Hank, and Hank was influenced by Myron*. The casual listener would think that polka music sounds like polka music, and country music sounds like country music. Sometimes, though, you have to pay closer attention to catch the nuances. Sometimes you have to dig a bit deeper.

The truth is, polka and country are distant cousins. One of the reasons the genres' stylistic similarity isn't too obvious to the casual listener is that, tempo-wise, they're radically different, polka generally being much faster than country. But country and polka dovetail together when it comes to the chord movement, as well as the overall tone and spirit.

This artistic parallel is probably why, as a kid, I took to country music. I mean, songs like Ray Price's "Heartaches by the Number" and "Don't Let the Stars Get in Your Eyes" are *this close* to being polka, so how could I not like them? This is why, even today, I'm always on the lookout for country artists I'd never really heard much of, just like I was in 1970, when I discovered a singer who would one day change my life.

I heard a song on the local radio station called "Columbus Stockade Blues." Accompanied only by an acoustic guitar, the smooth-but-rough vocalist drawled about how he was incarcerated in a Columbus, Georgia, prison; all his friends had turned their backs on him, and he missed every minute he'd ever spent with his little darling. After the tune faded out into the sunset, the deejay explained that it was a traditional country song from the 1930s, originally recorded by a gentleman named Cliff Carlisle, and since covered by Woody Guthrie, Bill Monroe, and Doc Watson, among many others. This particular recording, hot off the press, was the title cut of an album from a newcomer by the name of Willie Nelson. I went out and bought the record the next day.

It turned out that I was ahead of the curve on Willie Nelson; thanks to that long-forgotten deejay, I was on to Willie before most of the rest of the world knew who he was. My respect and admiration for him went off the charts when, a couple of years later, I found out that he started out as a polka musician. (But you already knew that because he discussed it in his foreword to this book. Thanks again, Willie!) When I learned about his love for my music years later, I told myself, *If I ever meet him, I'm gonna ask him to record with me.*

Fast-forward to 1996. I found myself on a bill at a country music festival in Hunter, New York, a bill headlined by, you guessed it, Willie Nelson. Before our band went on, I noticed Willie's bus driver was standing around backstage, looking bored. I wandered over, introduced myself, explained who I was, then said, "I know Willie loves polka music and I want to get him into the studio with us. Can you help me out?"

The driver said, "After his show, Willie'll be signing autographs for an hour-and-a-half. When he's done, I'll bring him right back here, right back to this very spot, and I'll introduce you guys. When you meet him, you give him a firm handshake, look him right in the eye, and tell him exactly what you want."

I said, "I can do that."

Exactly ninety minutes after his performance, the driver brought Willie to the appointed area and introduced us. As

Jimmy and Willie on The Nashville Network.

ordered, I gave him my best handshake, made direct eye contact, and said, "Willie, I know you started out playing polka. Would you consider recording with our band?"

He smiled and drawled, "Welllllll, I'd like to do that. Let me give you my number." Right there, right on that spot, Willie Nelson, one of country music's living legends, handed me his phone number. Just like that. *Wow!*

A few months later, I went down to Austin, Texas, and laid down a few cuts with Willie for an album that was eventually titled *Polka! All Night Long*. The session was more pleasurable and rewarding than I could have ever dreamed; it was the beginning of a friendship that continues to this day. Willie has graced four more of my recordings; suffice it to say that he's welcome at any of my recording sessions—anytime, any place.

After *Polka! All Night Long* hit stores, I got a call from a programmer at The Nashville Network. "Jimmy, that new record of yours, well, we all love it up here. It has a country vibe, and I think our viewers would enjoy it, so we want you to come on our station . . ." he said.

I replied, "Great!"

". . . and bring Willie with you."

"Ah. Okay. I can't guarantee anything, but I'll ask him." After a pause, I asked, "If Willie won't do it, do you still want us?"

The TNN man said, "Um, yeah. Sure. Why not?"

I knew that a TNN appearance could garner us a whole new audience. I also knew from the TNN man's tone of voice when I asked if he'd have us without Willie that there was a 50 percent chance that if there wasn't a Nelson, there wouldn't be a Sturr. I wanted the job, so I tracked Willie down that very day.

After I posed the question, he drawled, "Welllllll, I'd like to do that." Little did I know that Willie *never* did The Nashville Network because he wasn't a fan of the Nashville machine as a whole. (Apparently, he never forgave Nashville producers for insisting that, when he was on the cusp of superstardom, he record with what he perceived to be a schmaltzy string section. Willie is too cool for schmaltz, so I can't say I blame him.) But he was going to do it for me. Again, *wow*!

As if that wasn't thrilling enough, the next day I received a call from a booker at the Grand Ole Opry in Nashville. Since 1925, the Opry's stage has been graced by the likes of Patsy Cline, Hank Williams, Bill Monroe, Ernest Tubb, Dolly Parton, Garth Brooks, Reba McEntire, Carrie Underwood, and Brad Paisley, among *many* others; the lengthy list is a veritable Country Music Hall of Fame. "We understand you're making an appearance on The Nashville Network in a couple of weeks," the booker said. "Would you be interested in doing a show here at some point that week?"

"Am I interested? Is the sky blue? Does a dog bark? Is Florida the Onion Capital of the World?"

"Wait, Florida? Onions? Is that a yes, Mr. Sturr?"

I told the booker, "Of course I'm saying, yes. You bet I'm interested! Wouldn't miss it for the world." Aside from the venue's prestigious history, the Opry wasn't known as the kind of place that hosted polka concerts on a regular basis, so I wanted in. Badly.

"Great. And, um, you know, if you want, you can bring Willie Nelson with you."

"Ah. I'll see what I can do." After a beat, I asked, "If I don't have Willie with me, do I still get the gig?"

"Um, yeah. Sure. I guess. Why not?"

His less-than-enthusiastic tone didn't inspire much confidence, so I said, "Okay. I'll ask Willie. I'll do my best."

I tracked down Willie that very afternoon, which was more than a little surprising, because Willie is one of the hardest working men in show business. After I made my pitch, he drawled, "Welllllllll, I'd like to do that. Tell me where to be, and I'll be there."

"Willie, from the bottom of my heart, I thank you."

"Welllllllll, it's my pleasure. And you know what? This'll be the first time I've done the Opry."

"Really?"

"Really. You know how I feel about Nashville."

Two months later, it was time. The TNN taping was on a Thursday evening; our soundcheck was scheduled for that same day, just before noon. Noon rolled around, but Willie was nowhere to be seen.

The producer said to me, "He's not coming."

"What do you mean, he's not coming?" I said. "He'll be here."

"No. He won't. He's done this to us before. A number of times. We're gonna try and get a replacement."

"What do you mean a replacement? We can't play with just *anybody*. Willie knows our music and he knows polka. You can't just pull in somebody off the street. It's not that easy . . ."

Two minutes into my calm, patient diatribe, we heard a scream from the other side of the studio: "WILLIE'S BUS JUST PULLED UP! WILLIE'S HERE! WILLIE'S HERE!"

The place came to a dead standstill and went dead silent—it was like somebody pulled a plug. A few seconds later, in walked the man himself, looking calm, relaxed, and glad to be there. On his way up to the stage, Willie shook every hand that was offered to him, moving slowly so he could deliver all the TNN staffers a smile or a kind word. When he finally made it over to us, he gave all my band members a hearty hello and then embraced me as if we were long-lost brothers. He then turned around, looked around the room, nodded, and said, "Welllllllll, I'm ready."

He wasn't lying. We tore that place up. And that was just the soundcheck.

The taping that night was a smashing success, both personally and artistically, and I say personally, because I was given a piece of advice that changed *everything*. After we wrapped up our performance, which was even more raucous than the soundcheck, one of the producers pulled me aside and said, "Jimmy, you've got a helluva band there. But you're never going to be anything more than you are until you step out front."

"What do you mean, step out front?" I asked. "I'm the bandleader."

He shook his head. "It's pointless to tell everybody you're called Jimmy Sturr and His Orchestra if nobody can tell who Jimmy Sturr is. The way you set up right now, you look like one of the boys and nothing more. When you guys play, you stand over there," he said, pointing to the row where I sat alongside the other saxophonists. "You need to stand over *there*," he insisted, then pointed to stage center.

"You think that'll make a difference?"

"Jimmy," he said, "I've been doing this a long time, and if there's one thing I've learned, it's that in order to succeed, the audience has to know exactly what they're getting, especially if they're not familiar with you or your music. It's your band. You need to make sure that everybody knows it."

I liked being one of the boys, but I understood his point, so when I got back to Florida later that week, I hired a saxophonist to take my place in the reed section, planted myself front and center, and never looked back. That was the one of the best pieces of advice I'd ever received. And it wouldn't have happened if Willie Nelson hadn't been part of my life. That producer's name was Bill Turner.

In any event, there was no time for us to rest on our laurels after the TNN deal because the next night we had to deal with the Grand Ole Opry.

In order to add some spice to the show, the Opry brain trust decided to keep Willie's appearance a secret, so we devised a plan to make his appearance somewhat dramatic. After three songs, I was going to sing the first part from one of the tunes from *Polka! All Night Long*, then Willie would stroll out from the wings and sing the rest. We asked Willie if that was okay with him, and he said, as he often did, "Welllllll, that sounds like fun to me." When he set foot on stage, the audience let out a collective scream that was so loud, we were unable to hear another note for the rest of the tune. It was like he was Elvis, all four Beatles, and Justin Bieber, all wrapped up in one long-haired, cowboy hat–wearing package.

I consider the fact that I played a small role in Willie Nelson's triumphant debut at the Grand Ole Opry one of my great career highlights. But we can't talk about career highlights without talking about Farm Aid.

When Willie Nelson, John Mellencamp, and Neil Young put together the first Farm Aid festival in 1985, I don't think they could have possibly imagined what it would become. Sure, that first concert in Champaign, Illinois, which featured the likes of Bob Dylan, B.B. King, Billy Joel, and Roy Orbison, was a rousing success, raising some nine million dollars for struggling farmers all over the United States, but did they envision that Farm Aid would become an American fund-raising force for almost three decades? I doubt it, but it did. And congratulations to them.

Being that Florida, New York, was filled with onion farmers who struggled almost as often as their Midwestern brethren, I was well aware of Farm Aid. So when Willie asked me to

Opposite top: Taken at Farm Aid, Jimmy, Jesse Jackson, and Willie in Willie's tour bus during a break.

Opposite bottom: Backstage at Farm Aid—Jimmy with John Mellencamp.

perform at the 2005 show in Manassas, Virginia, I was honored and thrilled and excited. At that point Farm Aid was iconic, and being associated with something so huge was like getting a seal of approval from the mainstream music industry. Not only did Willie ask the band to perform but I was also invited to appear on a pre-festival panel with Willie, Neil, John, and Dave Matthews. My ensuing two Farm Aid experiences were equally amazing, but nothing can top that first year.

When Willie was at Farm Aid, he was obviously the center of attention, always getting pulled this way and that, but no matter how busy he was, no matter how many interviews he had on the books, no matter how many hands he had to shake, no matter how many farmers he stopped to hug, he always made it a point to perform a song with us, which is further proof that Willie Nelson is one of the finest gentlemen you'll ever meet, either inside or outside the world of music.

Postscript: *A couple years after we met, Willie and I were sitting on his bus, chatting about nothing in particular, when he pulled out a joint and asked, "Care for some?" As mentioned earlier, I have never indulged. I don't think there's anything wrong with it, it's just not my cup of tea. I gave Willie a thanks-but-no-thanks. Over the following few years, that scene repeated itself numerous times until one afternoon, when he gave me one of his trademark grins and said, "Welllllll. I hear ya, Jim, I hear ya. But someday, someday I'm gonna get ya!"*

To this day, he hasn't gotten me, but knowing Willie, he'll keep trying . . .

17

More Special Guests, Part One

Willie wasn't the first country music heavyweight who graced one of my albums—that honor would go to my old friend "Whispering" Bill Anderson—but you could say that having Willie on my CD legitimized me in the eyes of the country world, so I was comfortable asking other country folks to join me in the studio. Mel Tillis, for instance.

Mel, who'd climbed atop the country charts with such tunes as "I Ain't Never," "Good Woman Blues," "Heart Healer," "I Believe in You," "Coca-Cola Cowboy," and "Southern Rains" had a little theater of his own in Branson, Missouri, so he was easy enough to find. The process was pretty simple: I wrote him a letter asking him to record, and he wrote back with a yes. He came down to the studio and laid down some brilliant vocals on "San Antonio Rose," our polka'd-up rendition of the classic originally recorded by Bob Wills and the Texas Playboys.

If I may digress for a moment (and if you've read this far, you're used to my digressions), I'd like to offer a melancholy little story about "San Antonio Rose." There was a hugely popular TV show out of Austria called *Musikantenstadtl*, hosted by a gentleman named Karl Moik. Karl was a big fan of our band, and in June 2001, he invited us to play on an edition of the show they were shooting out in New York City. When we got to the set—a café right under the Brooklyn Bridge—the producer told me that I'd be lip-synching "San Antonio Rose." Now I'd never lip-synched anything in my life, but I was game, even though I'd be mouthing Mr. Tillis's verses.

Before we got started, the director had the cameramen position themselves so viewers would be able to see the entire New York skyline over our shoulders, a skyline that still included the World Trade Center towers. When the show aired in Europe in late September of that year, there were the Twin Towers in the background. I'm sure it was tough for some of the viewers to see the now fallen buildings, but there's a part of me that's pleased Jimmy Sturr and His Orchestra was documented on film with the New York skyline looking the way it always looks in my dreams.

And now we continue on a less melancholy note.

Mel Tillis and Willie Nelson represent merely the tip of my country iceberg. My friend Doyle Brown, who worked as a song pusher for Lawrence Welk Publishing, was a great help in introducing me to artists, including The Oak Ridge Boys. (Song pushers, by the way, help connect songwriters with recording artists, and Doyle was close to the Oaks because he introduced them to Sharon Vaughn, who wrote their first hit, "Y'all Come Back Saloon.") The Oaks were some of the nicest guys you'll ever want to meet, and I was especially thrilled when the album they guested on, *Dance with Me*, won a Grammy. I sure hope they were just as thrilled!

Some of my special guests weren't the least bit famous and were happy to stay in the background. One of them in particular became a key component in our day-to-day existence. And he was, of all things, an arranger.

I'd been writing the majority of my band's arrangements since the beginning and when I say the beginning, I mean the *beginning*, all the way back to my teenage days with the Melody Makers. Now, I wasn't a great arranger, but I got the job done. Deep down, however, I knew that there was somebody else out

Jimmy and the Oak Ridge Boys together on The Nashville Network. They had just finished recording an album together.

there who could bring these harmonies and melodies to life with more skill and imagination.

Enter Henry Will.

Henry—who was born Henry Wilczynski—was one of the finest accordion players in all of Connecticut, but he played more than polka. If you had a classical piece, a rock tune, or a country melody that needed a splash accordion, Henry could nail it on the first take, without fail. He played in a number of the best bands in the area, most notably that of Walt Solek's. (An interesting fact about Henry: He was Richard and Karen Carpenter's first piano teacher, so you could say that without Henry Will, we might not have enjoyed such pop classics as "Rainy Days and Mondays," "Close to You," or "Superstar.") I eventually found out that in addition to being a terrific musician, Henry was also one heck of an arranger. He had contributed both material and accordion and piano lines to the repertoires of numerous Connecticut polka heavyweights. Which got me thinking—if Henry's arrangements were good enough for the Walt Soleks of the world, then they were damn sure good enough for me. One phone call later, I was the proud owner of a dozen of Henry's masterworks.

I don't know whether it was a matter of timing or musical synergy, but when we added Henry's arrangements to our book, things started popping for Jimmy Sturr and His Orchestra. Something about the way he put together these songs captured our fans' imaginations. There was a sense of naturalness about his charts, and they were so solid that we felt comfortable sight-reading them on the bandstand. In other words, we would often perform them live without having previously rehearsed them. (At times, my arrangements felt forced, and I'd never play one of them during a concert without having had run through them at a rehearsal or three. Heck, I still have nightmares about listening to the same record over and over and over again, trying to figure out what part the saxes should play, what I should give to the trumpets, and the best way to stay true to the original song while making it appeal to our listeners. It took me forever, but Henry could do it in his sleep.) As of 2012, Henry and I are still happily working together. Matter of fact, as soon as I finish writing this chapter, I'm going to get on the phone with him and start figuring out what's going on the next Jimmy Sturr and His Orchestra CD!

Henry wasn't the only person who padded our book. Once in a rare while, another great arranger would fall into my lap.

I've always been a huge fan of a group called Danny Davis and the Nashville Brass. At some point in the mid-1960s, Danny, a trumpeter/vocalist who'd had a couple of hits in the 1950s with "Object of My Affection" and "Crazy Heart," decided he wanted to put together a band that would perform instrumental versions of country music hits. The band was a smash, nabbing both a Grammy Award—and was nominated for eleven others—and a regular slot on the TV show *Hee Haw*.

I was lucky enough to perform a few shows with Danny and his crew, and I was always quite impressed with his drummer, Terry Waddell. When Danny semiretired, Terry moved to Branson, Missouri, where he filled the drum chair for Bobby Vinton's band. Terry was an excellent arranger in his own right, so I asked him to fill out the remainder of our book with clever instrumental versions of American pop, rock, and country hits by the likes of Steve Miller, Stevie Ray Vaughan, and the Allman Brothers. (Sometimes the folks who hired us to perform at their wedding needed a dose of something of the non-polka variety, and I like to keep the paying customers happy.) Henry and

Terry's combined talents are one of the reasons I've been able to keep my shows and records fresh and exciting. I would advise all of you up-and-coming bandleaders to lock down a terrific arranger or two. You, your listeners, and your future record producers will thank me.

18

How to Polka-ize
a Non-Polka, or More
Special Guests, Part Two

It may seem simple to take a song like Steve Miller's "Swingtown" and turn it into a polka, but I personally believe there's an art to it. If it were easy, I suspect more musicians would be doing it, because there are a whole lot of folks out there who would enjoy it.

Step one: figure out the proper tempo. You might have to slow it down, or more likely speed it up because your typical polka song is generally faster than your typical rock tune. But you can't speed it up *too* much because there's the danger that it'll sound like a train going downhill without brakes. That rollicking speediness can be exciting, but there's a time and a place for everything.

Step two: figure out the logical way to deliver the melody. Sometimes it makes sense to sing the song, but often it's better to perform it as an instrumental. In my band, we mix it up. Sometimes I'll sing lead, sometimes I'll sing harmony, sometimes I'll play the melody, and sometimes I'll play a background riff. I'll do whatever best serves the material, because when you're covering somebody else's big hit, you're better off making it about the song rather than the performance.

Step three: try and recruit the original artist to perform the song. This isn't always easy, and when you're doing the asking, it generally helps to have a couple of Grammy Awards to your name. Having said that, it's always worth trying, because the worst thing that can happen is the artist will say no. The chances that somebody's going to smash you over the head with a guitar simply for asking a question are very, very slim.

I've never been afraid to ask, especially if the song will be better served if the singer/composer joins us in the studio. For example, we came up with an arrangement of Duane Eddy's "Rebel Rouser," a song I've always loved; once I realized that we *had* to record it, I asked the folks at Rounder Records if they could find out if Duane was still alive. It took a few phone calls for them to learn that Duane was still among the living, situated in Nashville.

At that point, I took over.

I looked his name up in the Nashville phonebook—yes, he was listed—gave him a ring, and invited him into the studio. He said, "Jimmy Sturr, I know all about you. My wife and I have seen you on The Nashville Network. Just tell me what time to be at the studio, and I'm there." Next thing you know, Jimmy Sturr and His Orchestra, with special guest Duane Eddy, cut the world's first polka-ized version of one of my favorite rock classics.

Grammy-winning country great Lee Greenwood, the man who recorded such hits as "God Bless the U.S.A.," "Dixie Road," "Don't Underestimate My Love for You," and "Hearts Aren't Made to Break (They're Made to Love)," was another singer who graced one of my records, and our meeting was a serendipitous one: We were both performing, and therefore staying, at the Mohegan Sun casino up in Connecticut. I ran into him in the lobby and on the spur of the moment, invited him to the studio. Much to my surprise, without even batting an eye, Lee said, "I'd love to." More proof that it never hurts to ask.

And then there was blues/rock singer/multi-instrumentalist Delbert McClinton, a wonderful live performer who hit it big in 1980 with "Giving It Up for Your Love."

And then there was my former labelmate at Rounder, the lovely Alison Krauss.

And then there was Charlie Daniels, who agreed to come by after a three-minute phone call.

And then there was Béla Fleck, the astounding banjo player I met at my first trip to the Grammy Awards.

And then there was my old favorite Ray Price, a country giant among giants who, as of this writing, is still touring and recording at the tender age of eighty-something.

And then there was Frankie Ford, the self-proclaimed "New Orleans Dynamo" who helped make *Shake, Rattle, and Polka!*, well, dynamic.

And then there was the legendary Arlo Guthrie, who joined us on a version of "City of New Orleans," one of my favorite songs, a song so poignant that it was recorded by everybody from Willie Nelson and John Denver to Judy Collins and Jimmy Sturr.

And then there was Bobby Vinton, a big fan and great friend of mine who, for some reason, took a lot of convincing before he'd join us in the studio. (It was a heck of a lot easier to get him to write his foreword for this book than it was to get him behind a microphone!)

And there was Brenda Lee, who beautified the studio when she appeared on one of our records with Willie Nelson. Talk about star power!

I'm grateful to each and every one of these artists, but there are still a number of other singers I'd like to work with. Off the top of my head, k.d. lang comes to mind, because from what I've heard, she's a huge polka fan. But my white whale would be Bob Dylan, and landing him may not be as unrealistic as you might think, because he recently cut himself a polka tune. So k.d. and Bob, if you're reading this, please get in touch!

Bob Dylan and k.d. lang aren't the only artists I'd love to get into the studio, but in terms of big stars, they're the most realistic. Those two folks aren't out of the question, but there are some others who are long shots. It probably won't surprise you to hear that Steve Miller is right near the top of that list. On the surface, that might not make sense. You might not envision "Jungle Love" or "Fly Like an Eagle" performed with that 2/4 beat. But from what I know of his music, I suspect Steve enjoys a good polka, so you never know.

One gentleman who might be a bit harder to nail down than any of these people is Elton John. Elton is an even less likely polka subject than Steve Miller, but he's a showman; for me, one of the most important aspects of a good polka concert is show-manship. Our band doesn't merely take the stage, play the songs, and then leave. We want to entertain you. After all, you set your night aside, you've gotten a babysitter, and you've driven all the way to the show, so the least we can do is give it our all. I can see Elton, right there next to us, doing everything in his power to get the crowd dancing. The only problem might be the clash of styles. Every once in a while, Steve Miller throws a little bit of country into his blues/rock (and as you know by now, country and polka are the perfect marriage), but I've never heard a single note from Elton John that would suggest he'd know what to do with a polka. But I'd sure love to hear him try.

Here's a name that might surprise you: Lady Gaga. Now, if I'm really honest, I don't know all that much about Lady Gaga's music, but from what I've seen of her performances on the Grammy Awards, she has as much showmanship as Elton John. (As a matter of fact, one of her Grammy appearances features her playing alongside Elton, and from my perspective, she "outshowmanshipped" him.) I have a gut feeling that there are a good number of people in Gaga's enormous international audience who, even though they might not know what polka is, would enjoy it. After all, polka is, first and foremost, a type of dance music.

As you can see, I'll happily welcome all comers who want to dabble in polka: soul crooners, jazz instrumentalists, rock shouters—anyone. If you want to give it a shot, the doors to my recording studio are always open. And if you join us, all you have to do is show up on time, sing in tune, give it your all, and have a great time.

Jimmy taking a break with Burt Reynolds, who is a huge fan of Jimmy's music.

19

The Music City

For a variety of reasons, Nashville is one of my favorite places on Earth. To explain why, I'll need to tell you about a Kentucky native by the name of Billy Vaughn. You're probably wondering why I'm starting a conversation about Tennessee with a mention of Kentucky. Well, as always, there's a method to my madness.

Billy Vaughn was one of the greatest arrangers of pop music that this country has ever seen. He had countless hits, including renditions of "Hawaiian War Chant," "Sail Along Silvery Moon," and "A Swingin' Safari." Vaughn's arrangements had a distinct sound, the most notable quality of which was his use of lead alto saxophones. While most arrangers of his day—or any day, for that matter—tended to highlight their brass section, Billy used the saxophones like no one else—especially the altos—so when you heard a Billy Vaughn tune, you *knew* it was a Billy Vaughn tune.

Naturally, as a saxophonist I always liked that sound, so I asked my pal Danny Davis if he'd be upset if I did an album called *Jimmy Sturr and the Nashville Saxes*, which was a riff on the name of his famous band, the Nashville Brass.

He said, "Upset? Are you kidding? Hell, I'll even produce the damn thing for you! You can record it down by us, here in Nashville. And if you supply the saxophonists, I'll supply the rhythm section."

So I called up Vern Whitlock, the other alto saxophonist in our band, and a couple of the other guys in our group, and we made the trip down to Nashville, where we cut the record at Porter Wagoner's Fireside Studio, a record that turned out to be one of my all-time favorites. It turned out to be one of Porter's favorites, too; he liked what he heard so much that he contributed a wonderful vocal turn on an old Hank Williams song called "I'm So Lonesome, I Could Cry," and then, after we finished recording, he kept Vern and me awake until four in the morning, adding sax riffs to some of his old arrangements. Over the ensuing years, Porter became one of my closest Nashville pals, yet another reason why the Music City holds a special place in my heart. (My apologies if it seems like I'm dropping names, but interacting with these country music legends is something that I'll proudly trumpet to the world from now until the end of time.) I felt so comfortable at Fireside that a couple of years later, I hauled the entire group down to Nashville, and over a four-day span, we recorded enough material for three albums.

This wasn't the first time that Danny helped me bring one of my musical visions to life. Several years before, I'd casually mentioned to him how much I enjoy the background vocalists who seem to show up on all the Nashville-based records of the era; all those perfectly harmonized *oohs* and *aahs* were always the cherries and whipped cream on top of the country music sundaes I so enjoyed indulging in.

Danny said, "You like that stuff? You know what? That gives me an idea. Let's get you into to RCA Studios." Sure enough, he set me up with a quartet of background vocalists who recorded with the likes of Elvis Presley and Hank Snow, and not only that, but the engineers for those sessions were legends in their own rights: Tom Pick and Roy Shockley.

Roy Shockley was Chet Atkins's brother-in-law—Chet was one of the great producers and even greater guitarists in country music history. He oversaw sessions by everybody from Elvis to Waylon Jennings and Dolly Parton and won fourteen Grammys of his own. Roy himself had twiddled the knobs for Willie Nelson, among *many* others. Tom Pick is no slouch either—he'd worked with many of the same artists as Roy and Chet, in addition to Perry Como, Guy Clark, and "Skeeter" Davis. From the second I met them, I could tell that these guys were the best of the best, and I knew that they'd make me sound better than I'd ever sounded. And I was right. Better yet, as was the case with Porter, Tom became one of my dearest friends and musical partners in crime. When I'm in the studio, I don't want anybody but him behind the mixing board. He's that good.

And speaking of Elvis, when some people think about the "King of Rock and Roll," they think about his Vegas days and that white sequined jumpsuit. Others remember all his movies, like *Blue Hawaii*, or *King Creole*, or *Girls! Girls! Girls!*, while some recall his early-career material, where he was more of a blues shouter than a rock-and-roll singer.

I, however, have a special place in my heart for his recordings with The Jordanaires.

The Jordanaires were a vocal group that originated way back in 1948. Elvis recruited them in 1955, after seeing them perform with another country music giant, Eddy Arnold. The group (whose lineup was always a revolving door and, at various times over its five-plus-decade career, featured, among many others, Hugh Jarrett, Culley Holt, Ray Walker, Hoyt Hawkins, Bill Matthews, Gordon Stoker, Duane West, and Louis Nunley) joined Elvis in the studio, where they backed him up on "Heartbreak Hotel," "I Got a Woman," and "Money Honey." Over the next decade or so, The Jordanaires helped turn many of Elvis's good songs into *great* songs.

Tom Pick knew how much I loved the band's sound, so using one of his many connections, he tracked down The Jordanaires and hired the band to back me up. The Jordanaires graced thirty or so of my albums, and I think those guys enjoyed having me as much as I enjoyed having them.

So now you know why Nashville is one of my favorite places on Earth.

20

Boots, Myron, & Whispering Bill

O f all the musicians I've toured with, three stand out: "Boots" Randolph, Myron Floren, and "Whispering" Bill Anderson. They come from very different musical walks of life, so it stands to reason that I hooked up with them in very different ways.

First, meet Boots.

Reaching back to my roots as a concert booker, for the longest time I organized polka weekends at what was then the Playboy Resort in McAfee, New Jersey, where I'd hire a nationally recognized artist to play at the main theater while I'd do a show in one of the smaller rooms. I set the stipulation that whichever group was playing in the main theater would have to come by after their 8 p.m. performance and sit in during our 10:30 show. (Actually, our show wasn't a show so much as it was a huge dance party that sold out each and every night.) Danny Davis and Brenda Lee were among my favorite guests, but my favorite among the favorites was Boots Randolph.

Boots, whose birth name was Homer Louis Randolph III, was a native of Kentucky who, from the early 1960s until his death in 2007, was one of the main go-to studio saxophonists in Nashville. He recorded with Elvis Presley, Roy Orbison, Al Hirt, Brenda Lee, and REO Speedwagon, but he was best known for his classic single "Yakety Sax," a song that eventually reached iconic status when it was used as the theme to *The Benny Hill Show*.

In a lucky turn of events, several Northeastern promoters booked Boots's and my bands on a number of double bills, and we became great friends. I got comfortable enough with him to ask if he'd be interested in playing with us at our annual Christmas show in New York City. Now, nailing down musicians to play during the holidays is a hit-or-miss proposition—they either have a high-paying gig on the books or want to spend time with their families—but Boots, without the slightest hesitation, said yes. I was thrilled to have him aboard and wanted him to be as comfortable as possible, both musically and personally, so I wrangled copies of the arrangements he performed with his own band. All Boots had to do was show up and play the tunes he'd played hundreds of times. He enjoyed himself so much that over the ensuing years, he joined us at four more holiday shows.

Boots eventually toured with us for a while. (Whenever we had him in tow, we were always billed as Jimmy Sturr and His Orchestra, with special guest Boots Randolph). But the highlight of my association with the affable Mr. Randolph was our polkaized recording of "Yakety Sax" on *Let's Polka 'Round*. As we listened to the playback, Boots turned to me, gave me a huge smile, and said, "I've recorded this song at least a hundred times, and this is by far the best version I've ever heard."

Second, meet Myron.

From my first concert at that infamous PTA meeting back in Florida, I never had any illusions about my place in the music pantheon. I knew I'd never have a number-one hit. I was certain I wouldn't headline a sold-out show at Madison Square Garden. I seriously doubted I'd be flown to England by private jet for a royal command performance. But the one thing I always believed was within my grasp was hosting a television show. I figured, if Lawrence Welk could do it, so could I.

My parents loved *The Lawrence Welk Show*, and every Saturday night, we'd park ourselves in front of the TV and watch Welk lead his orchestra through the "Great American Songbook." I generally only watched until the show's halfway point, because once I saw Myron Floren, I was set.

Myron, who, thanks to Lawrence, was known to his fans as "The Happy Norwegian," was arguably the best-known accordion player of his generation. In 1950 Welk stole Myron away from a band called the Buckeye Four, and for the next thirty-two years, Myron was both his main soloist and assistant conductor, and his feature in the middle of every show was, for many, its highlight. Eventually, he went on to lead his own ensemble, the Myron Floren Orchestra, with which he brought polka to the masses.

I first met Myron in the late 1970s, when my band backed him up at one of his concerts (he didn't always tour with his full orchestra), and we bonded right off the bat, both personally and musically. Not only could he play the heck out of that accordion of his but he was a good guy. A joy to perform with, Myron could always read an audience and pick the exact right song for the exact right moment, a feat that's not nearly as easy as you might think. Myron and I got on so well that I invited him to join us on stage at Carnegie Hall; the show went so well that we took the Carnegie stage together more times than I can remember. Our personal and professional relationship was so good that it got to the point that whenever Myron toured the Northeast, he hired us to back him. On more than one occasion, he told our audience, "Playing with Lawrence Welk was the most important thing I've ever done in my life, but let me tell you, this band behind me today, led by my friend Jimmy Sturr, is the second-best band I've ever performed with." We were lucky enough to make music with him until he passed away in 2005.

Country singer Bill Anderson and Jimmy clowning around at Soundshop Recording Studio in Nashville.

Before Myron passed, he gave me almost all of his arrangements, and almost all of them are still part of our repertoire. And whenever we play a Myron-ized tune, I always give him credit, because without Myron Floren, I might not be doing what I'm doing.

Third, meet Whispering Bill.

James William Anderson III, better known to his millions of fans as Whispering Bill, was a hit-making machine. Between 1962 and 2011, Bill released approximately fifty albums, thirty-two of which found their way onto *Billboard*'s country music chart. (That's such a staggering statistic, I feel it's necessary to repeat it: fifty albums, and thirty-two of them charted. Wow!) Those albums produced sixty-eight singles, all of which similarly charted. As amazing as the numbers for his albums are, those singles figures are mind-blowing. To break it down, each and every one of Whispering Bill's singles made it into the top one hundred, and of those sixty-eight, twenty-seven of them hit the top ten. And of those twenty-seven, five hit number one, those being "Mama Sang a Song," "Still," "I Get the Fever," "My Life," and "World of Make Believe." Even if you've never heard a note the man sang (or whispered), you have to be impressed.

I remember in the late 1970s, at a show in Middletown, New York, he performed "How Married Are You, Mary Ann," which was one of my favorite of his tunes and a nice little ditty that I thought would make for a wonderful polka. A few months after the Middletown show, I called him up and said, "You know, one of my favorite songs of yours is 'How Married Are You,' and I was wondering if—"

Before I could get the question out of my mouth, he said, "If you like it that much, record it."

I told him, "I'll record it if you sing it."

"Okay. Done deal."

That's Bill in a nutshell: easygoing, affable, talented, and willing to help. Little wonder he's another one of those guys who I'll be pals with until the end of time.

21

Don't Look for the Union Label

In theory, the American Federation of Musicians is a wonderful thing. In exchange for a member's yearly dues, it makes sure that the musician is treated well on his jobs, that he gets paid on time, that he's given the best possible deals, and that he's protected when a record label tries to screw him out of his royalties. This is why I joined the union the second I was old enough; for decades I was a member in good standing. I paid my dues on time, I regularly filed my paperwork, and I never spoke an ill word about the organization.

Unfortunately, the union wasn't nearly as good to me as I was to it.

I wasn't your normal union member, mind you, because I was more than a musician—I was also a bandleader and a promoter. This became problematic during one of those gigs at the Playboy Resort in McAfee, New Jersey. We'd been contracted to play there twice a year—once in March and once in November—a contract that had been renewed time and again because we sold out almost every show. But since Playboy treated us quite well, I was happy to be locked in.

About ten years into our tenure, Playboy sold the resort to Americana Hotels. When my union rep called me with the news, he said, "Look, we don't know what the hell Americana is going to do about your contracts now. They probably won't honor them."

I looked at my calendar and asked, "What about the show on Saturday, March 15?" It was only two weeks away.

"That one's fine."

"And the November date?"

"Don't know. Probably canceled."

There was a lot riding on those gigs, both financially and professionally, and the last thing I wanted was for them to dry up. "Is there anything you can do about it?" I asked.

"Maybe. Don't know. We'll see."

"Well, could you—" But before I could ask him my next question, he hung up.

The next morning, there was a rude knock on my office door. "Open up, Mr. Sturr! It's the police! We need to speak with you!"

As far as I knew, I hadn't done anything outside of the law, but when the law comes knocking, you can't help but get nervous. I opened the door and stammered to the four uniformed officers, "C-c-c-c-c-can I help you, gentlemen?"

One of them pulled out his badge and said, "Officer Kirk Upton, Philadelphia P.D. We'd like to book you and your band for a show up in the Catskills. We're having a departmental party, and a lot of the boys down there like the polka."

After my heart started beating properly again, I said, "Sounds great, officer. What date are you thinking?"

"Saturday, November 15."

I smiled and said, "Well, sir, it so happens that that day just freed up. We're in." I wrote up a contract, which he signed on the dotted line and then he headed back to Philly.

The following week, the phone rang; it was my contact from Playboy. "Well, Jimmy," he said, "it looks like the Americana people want you for those November shows."

"You're kidding."

"I'm not."

"I thought they weren't going to rehire us. I took on another job."

"I guess you'll have to get out of it."

I sighed, said, "I guess you're right," then, after I hung up with Playboy, I called my uniformed friend in Philadelphia and told him, "Listen, something came up, and I can't play on that Saturday night. I can play anytime on Friday, or on Saturday afternoon, or anytime on Sunday, but just not Saturday night at nine."

"We need you on Saturday night." All of a sudden, his tone was very police-like.

I tried to explain the situation with the Americana people, but he hung up on me in midsentence. A couple weeks later, he sued me . . . through the union. And the union—an organization to which I'd given thousands of dollars, an organization about which I'd always said nothing but good things—took the side of the policemen. Eventually, it was determined that I had to pay the cops what I considered to be an unfair sum out of my pocket. I'd always been led to believe that the union was there to protect its members in situations such as this, *especially* since the union told me the Playboy contract was probably going to be null and void in the first place!

But the union wasn't done with me yet. The union folks had so much fun messing around with Jimmy Sturr, the bandleader, that they decided they should mess around with Jimmy Sturr, the promoter.

One of the bands I used to book regularly for those Playboy/ Americana gigs was a locally popular unit called Stanky and His Pennsylvania Coal Miner Polka Band. (Now *that's* a name.) Right before one of the November weekends, I found out that Americana sold the resort to another company; I lost track of who bought what from whom and when. I was told that the company would honor our contract for that November show, as well as the following March performances, but after that, it was up in the air.

When I broke the news to Stanky, he nodded and didn't say a word about it. He played the November show and didn't say a word about it. He played the March show and didn't say a word about it. The following November, I received a letter from the union, ordering me to pay Stanky for the canceled job.

I shouldn't have been surprised that the union took Stanky's side, but I was.

But that's not all.

Even though the union had hung me out to dry twice, whenever I performed at a union venue, I still filed a contract with them. Why? Because that's what you do, no matter how shabbily you'd been treated in the past. But one time—*one time,* mind you—before a show in Las Vegas, I forgot. (What can I say? When you're a bandleader and a musician and a promoter, once in a while things fall through the cracks.) The week after the gig, somebody from the Vegas union called my house—not my office, my house—and my mother picked up the phone.

"Who's this?!" the rep demanded. "Where's the polka guy? Where's Sturr?!"

"This is Jimmy's mother, and he's not here right now. He's at his office. Can I help you?"

"YOU BET YOU CAN HELP ME, JIMMY'S MOTHER! HE DIDN'T DO WHAT HE WAS SUPPOSED TO DO AND HE KNOWS HE WAS SUPPOSED TO DO IT, AND WE WON'T STAND FOR IT! YOU TELL YOUR SON THAT HE'S IN A HELLUVA LOT OF TROUBLE! HE'S GONNA BE BROUGHT UP ON CHARGES! YOU'D BETTER RELAY THAT MESSAGE, JIMMY'S MOTHER, AS SOON AS HUMANLY POSSIBLE!"

When she called me up at the office, her voice was trembling. "He was awful, Jimmy, just awful. And I gave him your number at the office. I'm sorry if you didn't want me to do that, but . . ."

"Don't worry, Mom," I said. "I'll take care of it."

The union rep reached me a few minutes later. "Mr. Sturr," he said, "I just got off the phone with your mother, and I've gotta tell you, she was quite rude."

"Let me tell you something, pal," I said, trying and failing to maintain my cool. "I don't care what you say to me and I don't care how you do your job, and I don't care how many people you've buried in the desert, but you do not speak to my mother that way. Now you call her and you apologize. Then we can discuss this contract business." I slammed the phone down.

A few minutes later, my mother rang me up. "So I got a call from that gentleman in Vegas," she said, "and he apologized for about ten minutes. He was quite nice about it."

A few minutes after that, the union rep called me back. "Listen, Mr. Sturr, I'm sorry about the way this all went down. We're all embarrassed about it, so as an apology, how about we consider the matter closed?"

The next day, I tore my union card into thousands of tiny pieces.

22

Teammates

Question: what do a dumpling company and a satellite television network from Tennessee have in common?

Answer: They've seen fit to welcome Jimmy Sturr and His Orchestra into their respective families. But before I elaborate on that tenuous, although legitimate, connection, let us consider the *pierogi*, a delicious dumpling made from unleavened dough and filled with potato or sauerkraut or ground meat or cheese or fruit most associated with Poland . . . just like polka. So it would stand to reason that an internationally recognized pierogi company would be quite interested in partnering with an internationally recognized polka band. All of which is why, in the mid-1990s, Mrs. T's asked me to be its national spokesman. Because it has been so good to me, I'm going to present Mrs. T's version of its company history. It's the least I can do . . .

From a Twardzik family staple to your family's table, Mrs. T has been Serving Up Smiles long before there was a blue box with her name on it. Yes, there really is a Mrs. T behind all those boxes of delicious Pierogies. In fact, it's Mary Twardzik's original recipe that started this successful business back in 1952.

Mary's son, Ted, spent his childhood watching, learning, and of course, tasting, as his mother and her friends made Pierogies for church suppers. After college, he spent a year working for an accounting firm before realizing this Polish specialty might have wider appeal. After all, if they did so well at church dinners, why wouldn't they be a family favorite everywhere?

Sticking to his Schuylkill (pronounced Skoo-kil) County roots, Ted returned home to Shenandoah, PA and started making Pierogies in the very same kitchen where he had grown up watching his mother cook. Six weeks later, Mom asked him to move the mess elsewhere, and the rest is history. Ted set up shop in his father's former tavern and began churning out those potato-filled pasta shells by the dozen!

The company has expanded to many of the surrounding buildings over the years, but that tavern still remains a part of the Ateeco ("A 'T' [for Twardzik] Company") headquarters. Today, Ted's sons, Ted Jr. and Tom, look over the operation, which proudly employs nearly 230 people in its Pennsylvania plant. This makes Ateeco the largest employer in Shenandoah. With only 6,000 residents, this small town in Schuylkill County has made Ateeco the smiling success it is today!

Over 13 million Pierogies in 14 different varieties leave Ateeco's kitchens every week. That's over half a billion Pierogies a year! Whether it's feeding a small family dinner or large U.S. Military Commissaries overseas, Mrs. T's® has a size and a taste for everyone! For the family table, we sell our delicious Pierogies in package sizes of 12 and 24 in retail, convenience stores, and supermarkets. Larger counts of 48 and 72 are available for club and food service establishments, and Mini Pierogies come in 28 counts. From Shenandoah, Pennsylvania to Seattle, Washington, Mrs. T's® Pierogies are distributed coast to coast, Serving Up Smiles all across America.

Since we joined forces, the Mrs. T's crew has supplied us with our outfits, put me in a bunch of its television commercials, and supported us in every way the company can think of. In exchange, whenever our band is introduced, it's prefaced with "Mrs. T's Pierogies presents . . . ," and at some of our gigs, Mrs. T's sends a chef to give a pierogi-cooking demonstration. If there's one thing I've learned over the years, there's a whole lot you can do with a pierogi.

Believe it or not, after all these years, I still enjoy eating those little dumplings. And that's the absolute truth.

Now about that television station.

If you have DirecTV or the Dish Network, you might've seen my mug on your television screen because each and every Friday night, RFD-TV airs an episode of *The Jimmy Sturr Show*. For those of you who are strictly network television types, let me fill you in on what RFD-TV is all about.

Billing itself as "Rural America's Most Important Network," all of RFD-TV's shows fall into one of six categories: Agricultural, Equine, Rural Lifestyle, Music & Entertainment, Rural Youth, and Auctions. Of its Music & Entertainment selections, the network says:

> *Music has always been a part of rural America's heritage. It has long been a tie, binding family, friends and community together. Staying true to tradition, Music & Entertainment on RFD-TV focuses on the customs of rural lifestyle, showcasing its time-honored music, and classic pursuits.*
>
> *RFD-TV programs are sure to bring back fond memories from the past while continuing to bring in and create new, family-oriented entertainment that appeals to all generations.*

Now *that's* an attitude I can get behind.

Here's a confession about the show: I film them in batches of twenty over a five-day period. So if you do the math, that means

I end up shooting four shows a day, and that . . . is . . . *grueling!* Yes, it's unbelievably fun to perform with my band in front of the camera. Yes, it's a blast to have the opportunity to ham it up for the entire country. But making a television show—especially one right after the other—is about the hardest thing on my docket.

But it's worth it. It may not be *The Lawrence Welk Show* (Lawrence's act would be hard to top; plus, he was the pioneer in the music-television field, so to say I'm in his league is heresy), but it's a solid thirty minutes of entertainment. I'll talk for a bit, we'll have some guest singers and dancers, and, naturally, we'll play a lot of polkas. I like to mix things up, so one week we might focus on the trumpet, and the next, it'll be the accordion. The one constant is that it's always energetic, certainly more up-tempo than Welk. But additional speed is kind of a necessity; you see, we have to pop a bit harder than they did in the old days because today's viewers have a lot more options. Back then you had a choice between Welk, three other television shows, the radio, or a walk around the block. Today, there are about two million channels, the Internet, Netflix, and your latest iPad app. We need to grab your attention and hold on tight.

Musically speaking, I plan each show to the hilt, but in terms of my patter, I wing it, because if I scripted it, we might lose the spontaneity and energy that I believe puts us over the edge. That said, I still have a pretty good idea of what information needs to be conveyed and how I can convey it in the most entertaining, informative manner possible. Like Welk, I make sure that I regularly introduce the band, because one of the things I liked best about Lawrence's orchestra is that you *knew* everybody—you *knew* Myron Floren, you *knew* the Lemon Sisters—and that gave it the kind of communal feel that made viewers come back.

(A brief aside, still in the television world: In 2011 we recorded a TV special called *PBS Presents: Jimmy Sturr and His Orchestra.*

It was filmed at a hotel in Canada and was ultimately shown nationwide. The boost in our visibility was astounding.)

The band and I never get tired of doing our RFD-TV show, and hopefully the fine folks at RFD-TV will never get tired of us.

And speaking of the band . . .

23

Meet the Orchestra

I must be doing something right because some of the guys in my band have been with me for years. They're magnificent musicians; I'm sure they've had plenty of other opportunities to perform and/or record with other bandleaders, but they've stuck with me, and I'm the better for it.

For example, there's our drummer, Dennis Coyman. As of this writing, Dennis has been with me for almost forty years. It's possible there's a better polka drummer out there, and it's possible there's a better rock drummer or big-band drummer or country drummer, but I've never heard anybody who is able to do everything. Dennis can do it all.

Our lead trumpeter, Eric Parks, is another guy who's been with me for almost four decades. Eric was so dedicated to the band and our music that he managed to make our shows even when he was at West Point directing its band the Jazz Knights. That sometimes led to a bit of drama, because since he was in the army, he couldn't join the American Federation of Musicians. The union is pretty vigilant about making sure there aren't any nonunion musicians on any given stage. If we knew that there was going to be a union official in the area, Eric would wear some sort of disguise—a hat, for instance, or maybe some big sunglasses—so he wouldn't get himself (or us) in any kind of trouble. And as you know by now, you never want to mess around with the union.

Most of my orchestra members are from the Florida, New York, area; once in a while, however, I welcomed an import into the club. Tenor saxophonist/vocalist John Karas, for example, was in a polka band in his hometown of Buffalo, New York, and used to make it a point to see us whenever we rolled through, which, considering that Buffalo was a polka hotbed, was fairly often. After one show he told me, "Jimmy, I love Buffalo, but I *really* love your band. If I moved to your area, would you consider hiring me?"

I'd seen John play and sing in his own band, and the guy was terrific. I told him, "Yes. In a heartbeat. Move tomorrow." That was more than thirty years ago. He's been with us ever since. There's no better tenor sax player in the polka field, and possibly in the country.

Nick DeVito is an outstanding alto saxophonist/clarinetist; while he's a great polka player, he's one of the best jazz musicians to ever grace our bandstand. He's a wonderful improviser, too. If you give him a set of chord changes, he'll eat them up, regardless of the key or the complexity. Not every polka band in the world can say it has a guy like Nick.

And then there's our fiddler, Frankie Urbanovitch, who's been with the band for more than three decades. He's one of the more popular members of the crew, as witnessed by the enthusiastic fan emails we get for him after all of our television appearances.

Then there are the relative newcomers like trumpeter Kenny Harbus, who's been with us for a mere twenty-one years. Before joining the Orchestra, he sat in the first trumpet chair for the house band at the Concord Resort Hotel in the Catskills, which at the time was one of the largest hotels in the world. And there's our bassist, Richie Pavasaris, who's held down the bottom for just twelve years, and our piano player—the best keyboardist I've ever had—Keith Slattery, who has been tickling the ivories with us for fifteen years. (Keith's father grew up just down the street from me, and even though Keith and I played all kinds of sports together as kids, we didn't start making music together until we were all grown up.) Our Rhode Island–bred accordion player, Steve Swiader, has been part of the gang for a mere fifteen years or so; our Connecticut-bred trumpeter/singer, Kevin Krauth, has been with us for only nine years. Those newcomers might just stick. Without Steve and Kevin, the band would not be what it is today.

Our newest member is alto/clarinet player Jim Perry. What a great addition Jim has been. He, too, came from the Jazz Knights at West Point. Not only did he come from the Jazz Knights—he was the band's leader!

Now excuse me for a moment if I sound like a doting father, but do you want to know how good the guys in my band are? These days, we never rehearse. Never, ever, ever.

Whenever we have new material, I plop it on their music stands the night of the job. When they sight-read it, it sounds as if they'd been playing the tune for weeks. The second time through, they'll sound like they've been playing it for months; then, come the third pass, it sounds like they've been playing it for years. I *really* appreciate that, and they *really* appreciate that I *really* appreciate that, which is why the core of Jimmy Sturr and His Orchestra has remained intact for dozens and dozens of recording sessions, hundreds and hundreds of concerts, and will continue to do so until I can't pick up my clarinet.

AFTERWORD
Polka Today and Tomorrow

Something I've always appreciated about polka is that it never goes out of style. If you liked polka a million years ago when you were a kid, or if you like polka right now, chances are you're always going to enjoy our music, because no matter how you slice it or dice it, it's always going to be polka.

This isn't to say that polka music will remain stagnant, at least if I have anything to do with it. I'll always try to incorporate different styles and techniques into my band's book because I want to keep it fresh for my listeners and me. Yes, I love performing (looking at my tour schedule for the past few decades should make that obvious), but I still want to make it as exciting as possible. If that means bringing special guests into the studio or polka-izing a rock-and-roll hit from the seventies or standing on my head and playing my clarinet through my nose, I'll do it.

I've noticed over the last couple of years that our audiences are getting younger and younger. That doesn't surprise me because today's music listeners are more open-minded than people give them credit for. Some of today's most popular bands aren't exactly what they seem to be on the surface; if you dig a little deeper, you'll see some surprising influences. Let's take Adele, the terrific singer who took home all those Grammys in 2011. A casual listen tells us that she's a poppish soul singer, but if you go a bit deeper, you can hear traces of Aretha Franklin, Anita Baker, Ella Fitzgerald, Billie Holiday, and Janis Joplin. If you go up to a teenager who loves Adele, hand her a copy of *Ella Fitzgerald Sings the Cole Porter Songbook*, and explain that Ella is one of Adele's favorite singers, she would likely give it a listen. That kind of all-embracing attitude explains why, when you go to a performance by Jimmy Sturr and His Orchestra, it won't just be a roomful of old folks. We play to children of all ages. We further transcend generations when Chris Caffery, lead guitarist from the Trans-Siberian Orchestra, tours with us. He always brings the house down with his rock-like energy. When you add horns to that guitar, that adds up to one exciting sound, and those children of all ages, well, they go crazy.

One of the questions I'm most often asked is, "Do you want to win any more Grammys?" The answer is, of course, yes—if anybody answers no to a query like that, he's fibbing to both the questioner and himself—but awards aren't what drives me. All I'm concerned about is putting together good records, and if NARAS sees fit to honor me, that's wonderful. If not, I'll just do another record.

And another.

And another.

And another.

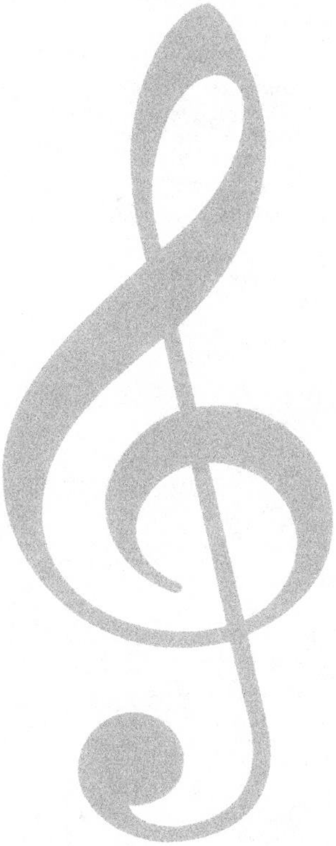

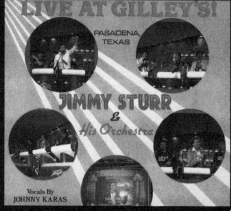

APPENDIX
Jimmy Sturr Selected Discography

1966
Polka Festival

1967
Jimmy Sturr and His Orchestra Stir Up a Musical Mix

1968
The Big Band Polka Sound
Polka Holiday

1976
Million Dollar Polkas
Ray Budzilek Meets Jimmy Sturr at a Polka Hop (with Ray Soyka)
Polka Fever
Happy Snappy Polkas (with Gene Wisniewski)

1977
Polka Saturday Night (with Gene Wisniewski)
All-American Polka Festival
Pure Polka (with Gene Wisniewski)

1978

Polkas (with Gene Wisniewski)

Jimmy Sturr and His Orchestra Play a Tribute to Ray Budzilek
    (with Gene Wisniewski)

Let's Have a Polka Party

A Polka Ride

Make Mine Polkas! (with Gene Wisniewski)

Polka Medley #6: Unita/Blue Eyes Crying in the Rain/Peanuts/Green Grass/
    Hosa Dyna/Down Yonder

1979

The Best of Jimmy Sturr

Polka Disco

This Is Polka Country! (with Gene Wisniewski)

1980

Country Polka

Legendary Golden Polka Favorites (with Myron Floren)

1981

Trip to Poland

Another Trip to Poland

1982

If You're Polish and You're Proud

Fiddles on Fire

1983

Pure Country (with The Nashville Saxes)

1984

Live! In Person at the Playboy Club

1985

Knee Deep in Polka Music

I'm Sturr Crazy

On Tour

1986

Sturr-i-Fic Polkas!

First Class Polkas! (with Myron Floren)

I Remember Warsaw (with The Jordanaires)

1987

Please Have Them Play a Polka Just for Me (with The Jordanaires)

The Greatest Hits of Jimmy Sturr and His Orchestra

1988

Born to Polka

1989

All in My Love for You

1990

Live at Gilley's!

1992

Sturr It Up (with The Jordanaires)

Presents Clarinet & Accordion Magic

A Jimmy Sturr Christmas

1994

The Best of Jimmy Sturr and His Orchestra, Volume 2

More Magic, Volume II

1995

Polka Your Troubles Away (with The Jordanaires)

Polka Favorites

1996

I Love to Polka (with The Jordanaires)

Polka! All Night Long (with Willie Nelson and The Jordanaires)

1997

Super Polka Party

Jimmy Sturr's Polka Favorites (with Myron Floren)

1998
Living on Polka Time (with Bill Anderson and Flaco Jiminez)
Touched by a Polka (with Mel Tillis)
Dance with Me (with The Oak Ridge Boys and The Rocco Sisters)
Life Is a Polka

1999
Polkapalooza (with Flaco Jiminez)

2000
Primetime Polkas (with Willie Nelson, Mel Tillis, The Oak Ridge Boys,
    The Jordanaires, Mel Tillis, and The Rocco Sisters)
83 Giant Polka Hits & Medleys

2001
Gone Polka (with Willie Nelson and Brenda Lee)
Jimmy Sturr Polka

2002
Top of the World (with Arlo Guthrie and Rhonda Vincent)

2003
Let's Polka 'Round (with Charlie Daniels, Béla Fleck, and "Boots"
    Randolph)

2004
Rock 'n' Polka (with Lee Greenwood, Duane Eddy, Willie Nelson,
    Alison Krauss, Larry Chance & The Earls, and Blue Highway)

2005
Grammy Gold

2006
Shake, Rattle and Polka! (with Willie Nelson, Delbert McClinton,
    Duane Eddy, Frankie Ford, and The Duprees)
The Greatest Hits of Polka (with Myron Floren, "Boots" Randolph,
    The Rocco Sisters, Mel Tillis, and Willie Nelson)

2007

Polka in Paradise (with Bobby Vinton)

Come Share the Wine (with The Jordanaires)

2008

Let the Whole World Sing (with Ray Price, Charlie Prose, and Raúl Malo)

2009

Polka Cola: Music That Refreshes (with Bill Anderson)

A Tribute to the Legends of Polka Music

Polka Party

2011

Not Just Another Polka

Legends of Polka Music

2012

Polka Is My Life

ACKNOWLEDGMENTS

First, a few special thank yous:

The first time I recorded in Nashville, my engineer was Tom Pick, a pairing set up by my friend Danny Davis, something that was a thrill, because at the time, Tom had thirty-two gold albums to his name. That was about forty years ago; today I consider him not only one of my greatest musical collaborators but one of my closest friends.

I met Chicagoan Keith Stras about thirty years ago, and he and I are great friends. He's done so much for me, both in and out of Chicago, and for that I'm eternally grateful.

Special thanks to Patrick Goetsch for making us a part of RFD-TV family.

In 1989 we were hired at what was then The Aladdin in Las Vegas, and the bookers asked me to bring aboard an opening band. I invited a group from Youngstown, Ohio, called the Joe

Fedorchak Orchestra. Joe's drummer was named Carmen White, and Carmen's cousin was named Joe Donofrio. Joe's wife, vocalist Kathy Rocco, and Kathy's singing sister Connie were performing at the same time. When they came to hear Carmen, they heard us; later that night, we returned the favor. Since then, Joe and Kathy have become among our closest business associates and among my closest friends. If you've ever heard my Orchestra perform at a casino, you can probably thank Joe.

I don't remember how I became friends with Tommy Lynch and his wife, Mona, but they're very, very special friends. Once in a while, Tommy will even drive our tour bus.

Tommy Conklin grew up across the street from me. About seven years ago, I asked him if he'd like to come on the road and give us a hand. He used to stand by the soundman, and he eventually picked up a few things, enough that he became an expert. To this day, Tommy travels the world with us, making certain we sound good.

Twins, former country singers, and associates of the Grand Ole Opry, Jack and Jerry Calhoun own two bus-leasing companies and supply buses to many of the biggest acts in the world. I hooked up with them back in the mid-1980s when I bought my first tour bus. The day we first met, Jack took me out to lunch. We then went back to his office, where he left me sitting alone for forty-five minutes. Eventually, concerned that I was going to miss my flight, I asked the secretary where he went. She told me, "Jack went golfing." Nonetheless, we're still great friends, and once in a while, I even let Jack and Jerry perform a couple of shows with us. Great guys.

Acknowledgments

Ben Gilman was our congressman for almost thirty years. He did so much for our area and is loved by just everybody. Over the last decade, we've made it a point to have dinner two or three times a week, and I cherish those meals.

Nobody has done more for me than my best friend, Gussie Koisor. Nobody's even come close. Without him, I'm not sure where I'd be. He's our band manager and our bus driver, as well as a partner in my record label, my travel agency, and my polka company, and takes care of business better than anyone ever could. We grew up together, played sports together, caused trouble together, and we'll be partners together until the end.

Thanks to Barbara James, Chris Caffery, Bill Anderson, Doug Ferony, Willie Nelson, John Michael Whitby, Mickey Raphael, Al Henson, Doyle Brown, all my former bandmates throughout the years, Joe Timmer, John Zobel, Arlene Alape, Charlie Wing, Tommy Gallagher, Terry Baker, Orville Slutsky, Ken Irwin, Ed Lehner, Austin James, Janine Adamczyk, Pete Roden, Valley Sturr, Kenny James, Jennifer James, Gene Muvahill, and Bobby Vinton. Also, a special thank-you to the team at BenBella Books, especially Glenn Yeffeth, Debbie Harmsen, Adrianne Lang, and Erin Kelley, as well as my literary agent, Steve Harris. In memoriam, I send my love to Dan Dempsey, Wes Oler, and Warren Bills.

And finally, nobody could ever ask for better parents. They stuck behind me in everything I ever did and always came to see the band play. They passed away when they were in their nineties; they're buried in a cemetery across the street from the house where I currently live (the same house in which I grew up), a lot that used to be Sturr property. They'll always be close to me both physically and in my heart.